33 DAYS TO DIVINE MERCY

MATTHEW KELLY

BLUE SPARROW BOOKS

Copyright © 2025
KAKADU, LLC
PUBLISHED BY BLUE SPARROW
AN IMPRINT OF VIIDENT

All rights reserved.
No part of this book may be used or reproduced in any manner whatsoever without permission except in the case of brief quotations in critical articles or reviews.

ISBN: 978-1-63582-572-5 (softcover)
ISBN: 978-1-63582-577-0 (eBook)
Audiobook available from Audible.

33 DAYS TO DIVINE MERCY
may be purchased for groups large and small.
For information, please call or email:
info@PilgrimsofMercy.com
1-859-980-7900
www.PilgrimsofMercy.com

International and foreign rights are available for this title.
For information, please email info@Viident.com
www.Viident.com

Divine Mercy Artwork
Brewww LLC
https://brewww.studio/

Designed by Todd Detering

10 9 8 7 6 5 4 3 2 1

FIRST EDITION

Printed in the United States of America

TABLE OF CONTENTS

INTRODUCTION

ONE MAN'S JOURNEY	1
OUR CULTURE'S NEED FOR MERCY	6
OUR PERSONAL NEED FOR MERCY	8
THE FOUR MOVEMENTS OF MERCY	9
WHAT IS CONSECRATION?	11
THE INCREDIBLE JOURNEY BEFORE YOU	12
THE HISTORY OF DIVINE MERCY	13
HOW TO USE THIS BOOK	17
LET THE PILGRIMAGE BEGIN	19

WEEK ONE: DIVINE MERCY AND THE PILGRIM

DAY 1	WHAT IS MERCY?	23
DAY 2	WHO IS MERCY?	25
DAY 3	A NEW BEGINNING	29
DAY 4	AN AUTHENTIC SENSE OF SELF	32
DAY 5	MERCY ISN'T EARNED	36
DAY 6	GENTLE KINDNESS	39
DAY 7	HUMILITY, HUMILITY, HUMILITY	42

WEEK TWO: DIVINE MERCY AND THE SAINTS

DAY 8	FAUSTINA: MERCY IS STRONGER THAN OUR MISERY	46
DAY 9	JOHN PAUL II: THE HAPPIEST DAY OF MY LIFE	50
DAY 10	AUGUSTINE: MORE BEAUTIFUL THAN EVER	53
DAY 11	MONICA: EVERY FAMILY NEEDS A PRAYERFUL GIANT	56
DAY 12	KATHARINE DREXEL: BE BOLD. BE CATHOLIC.	61
DAY 13	DAMIEN OF MOLOKAI: RADICAL COMPASSION	65
DAY 14	VINCENT DE PAUL: GOODNESS NEVER DIES	69

WEEK THREE: THE CORPORAL WORKS OF MERCY

DAY 15	FEED THE HUNGRY	73
DAY 16	GIVE DRINK TO THE THIRSTY	77
DAY 17	CLOTHE THE NAKED	81
DAY 18	SHELTER THE HOMELESS	85
DAY 19	VISIT THE SICK	90
DAY 20	VISIT THE IMPRISONED	93
DAY 21	BURY THE DEAD	98

WEEK FOUR: THE SPIRITUAL WORKS OF MERCY

DAY 22	INSTRUCT THE IGNORANT	102
DAY 23	COUNSEL THE DOUBTFUL	106
DAY 24	ADMONISH THE SINNER	110
DAY 25	BEAR WRONGS PATIENTLY	114
DAY 26	FORGIVE OFFENSES WILLINGLY	119
DAY 27	COMFORT THE AFFLICTED	122
DAY 28	PRAY FOR THE LIVING AND THE DEAD	125

THE FINAL DAYS: SURRENDER

DAY 29	WHAT IF?	130
DAY 30	THE SACRAMENT OF MERCY	133
DAY 31	BECOMING A PILGRIM OF MERCY	136
DAY 32	GIFT OF PEACE	139
DAY 33	JESUS, I TRUST IN YOU	143

APPENDIX:

THE DIVINE MERCY CHAPLET	152
THE DIVINE MERCY NOVENA	158
DIVINE MERCY AND THE SACRED HEART DEVOTION	169

ONE MAN'S JOURNEY

Mercy is love reaching out to misery.

It is impossible to understand yourself, or your life, or any other person, until you have discovered your own immense need for mercy. Until you have come to believe that the only thing greater than your need for mercy is God's desire to give it to you.

These discoveries will convince you and confront you. They will deepen your conviction that God wants you, and confront you with the ultimate question: Do you want God?

Let me begin with a story.

The year was 1725.

John Newton was born in London to a seafaring father and a devoutly Christian mother. His early years were a seesaw between spiritual instruction and premature worldly exposure. But his mother died while he was still young. This left him spiritually unmoored, his father took him to sea at the age of eleven, and rebellion quickly took hold of his life.

When he was nineteen, John was pressed into service in the Royal Navy. But he was allergic to the discipline and the following year he deserted the Navy, but was captured, flogged, and demoted to a common seaman.

Foul-mouthed, disobedient, and with an unrestrained penchant for debauchery, John was eventually discharged from the Navy and transferred to a merchant vessel engaged in the African slave trade.

He ended up in West Africa working for a slave trader named Amos Clowe. John's behavior and personality clashed with the captain, and over time, he fell into disfavor with Clowe and his African mistress, who wielded significant power.

This led John to become enslaved himself and subjected to horrendous abuse, deprivation, and forced labor. He was treated mercilessly, relied on scraps of food to survive, and out of spite, was made "a servant to the slaves," which underscored the depth of his suffering and humiliation.

It was around this time that news of John's plight reached his father in London, and he sent a ship to rescue his son.

On his voyage home to London, John awoke one night to the ship being ravaged by a vicious and violent storm. Everyone aboard was certain they were about to sink off the coast of Ireland. Wave after wave crashed down upon the ship and John saw one of his crewmates swept overboard, never to be seen again. So, tying himself to the ship's pump, he worked for hours to keep the vessel afloat. It was in a moment of desperation during this long night that he cried out to the God he had known as a child, "Lord, have mercy on us!"

This near-death experience became a pivotal moment in his life. This cry of desperation made John intensely aware of his great need for mercy. He would later credit this near-death experience with his spiritual awakening. But few lives can be drawn with straight lines, and his conversion was still years away.

Two weeks later, the battered ship limped safely into an Irish port. John and the crew were starving, but alive.

In the days and weeks that followed, John began to read the Bible and renew his relationship with Jesus. The seed of mercy was planted in his soul, but he struggled with feelings of unworthiness, which became an obstacle to his spiritual transformation.

Later in life, John would regret the fact that, having been liberated from slavery and saved that night from the storm on the high seas, he did not turn back to God completely. What did he turn to instead?

It may seem unbelievable at first, but John became the captain of a slave ship. He had experienced the brutal reality of slavery firsthand. He had personally been the victim of its dehumanization. And yet, he spent the next five years hauling free men, women, and children from Africa in the most inhumane circumstances so they could be sold into slavery in the Americas.

But all of that came to a halt at the age of thirty, when John suffered a massive stroke. He would never sail again.

The year was 1754.

What seemed like a tragedy at the time became the catalyst for one of the most famous spiritual conversions in the history of Christianity.

John was now forced to take an honest, unflinching look at the darkness of his past, and every aspect of his life up until that moment haunted him. His conscience was awakened to the horror of slavery and all the evil he had participated in. The faces of the men, women, and children he had forced into slavery tormented him night and day.

This led him deep into dark bouts of self-loathing. He hated what he had done and who he had become. He became deeply introspective and a desire for God rose up in him.

Each day he emptied himself in hours of prayer, throwing himself at God's feet, begging for mercy. But he considered himself unforgiveable and unworthy of God's love and mercy. And yet, by some extraordinary grace, he had the courage to keep showing up to prayer each day searching for light, hoping for hope.

He would eventually call it *Amazing Grace*.

The year was 1772.

These are the words this former slave trader penned to describe his quest for mercy and to honor his God after twenty-seven years of prayer and reflection. He wrote them to encourage you and me to believe in second chances and new beginnings.

Amazing Grace

Amazing grace! How sweet the sound
That saved a wretch like me!
I once was lost, but now am found;
Was blind, but now I see.
'Twas grace that taught my heart to fear,
And grace my fears relieved;
How precious did that grace appear
The hour I first believed.
Through many dangers, toils, and snares,
I have already come;
'Tis grace hath brought me safe thus far,
And grace will lead me home.
The Lord has promised good to me,
His Word my hope secures;
He will my Shield and Portion be,
As long as life endures.
Yea, when this flesh and heart shall fail,
And mortal life shall cease,
I shall possess, within the veil,
A life of joy and peace.
The earth shall soon dissolve like snow,
The sun forbear to shine;
But God, who called me here below,
Will be forever mine.
When we've been there ten thousand years,

Bright shining as the sun,
We've no less days to sing God's praise
Than when we'd first begun.

This once notorious slave trader underwent a profound spiritual conversion. John Newton allowed God's mercy to completely transform him. He became a minister, a renowned preacher, a champion of the abolitionist movement, and devoted his life to spreading the message of God's grace and the possibility of redemption.

Amazing Grace is the most popular hymn in the history of the world.

That's no small feat. There are a lot of great ones.

How Great Thou Art. Ave Maria. Holy, Holy, Holy! Lord God Almighty. Hail, Holy Queen. Panis Angelicus. On Eagle's Wings.

I have often heard *Amazing Grace* described as John Newton's greatest contribution. But I have to disagree. Let me explain. I love the hymn. I think it is extraordinary. I just don't think it was his greatest contribution.

The year was 1807.

A thunderous applause broke out in the courtroom. The British Parliament abolished the transatlantic slave trade by signing the Slave Trade Act of 1807. This victory for human rights was made possible by a small but tireless group of men and women.

John Newton was one of them.

This was his greatest contribution. Twelve generations have passed since 1807. That's twelve generations of Africans who were not sold into slavery. Twelve generations of men, women, and children who wake up to their ancestral homeland each day. Twelve generations of people who live in freedom. That's millions of people spared the unimaginable cruelty of slavery.

And not just twelve generations, but every generation in their bloodline going forward. That's tens of millions of people, maybe hundreds of millions of people, maybe billions.

A child is in her mother's arms tonight because of John Newton's efforts. Grandparents are playing with their grandchildren. Husbands and wives are sleeping side by side. Children are playing together outside their homes. Neighbors are laughing together. That's a tremendous amount of good, and a tremendous amount of Holy Moments.

Newton has been dead for 217 years. He died 271 days after the slave trade was outlawed. But for 217 years, the good he did has lived on.

The good we do lives on forever. The good we do never dies. It lives on in other people, in other places, and in other times. John Newton's goodness lives on today, and that is his greatest contribution.

The hymn, as magnificent as it is—and it is astounding—the hymn is just a dim reflection of his inner life, a dim reflection of his relationship with God. And when I reflect on that single idea, I am in awe wondering what that relationship was like. And the hymn, as crisp and as clear as it is, as glorious and elevating, the hymn is but a faint echo of John Newton's contribution.

The hymn, and the man, and his contribution to ending slavery, and his profound understanding of God's love and mercy—well, these are all just a dim reflection of the God he worshiped. Jesus Christ. The Lord of Mercy. The man and the mercy we are going to explore and encounter over the next thirty-three days.

OUR CULTURE'S NEED FOR MERCY

Imagine a world without mercy. Do you want to live in a society without mercy? I don't. And I don't want my children to grow into a world without forgiveness and second chances. But that's where our culture is headed. Cancel culture. An individual says or does something that the pack considers unacceptable, and that person is judged, criticized, rebuked, shunned, ostracized, fired from their job, and incessantly harassed on social media. There is no due process, there is no redemption, no chance to apologize and change your ways, no forgiveness, no second chances, and absolutely no mercy.

This mercy is essential if we are to learn to love each other again. There is no love without forgiveness. Without mercy all relationships fail eventually.

No culture or society can thrive without mercy. The more our culture abandons Christianity the more toxic and dysfunctional it becomes, and a world with no forgiveness would be a very toxic world indeed.

Our culture is aching for mercy. Our fractured relationships, the division and polarization within society, rising mental health challenges, extreme poverty, consumerism and self-centeredness, godlessness, increasing violence and crime are all calling out for mercy.

The need for God's mercy is more urgent than ever. We have made remarkable advancements in technology, science, and communication, and yet, we are struggling with moral and ethical ambiguity, social disintegration, and spiritual confusion.

We need to stop looking for worldly solutions to spiritual problems. The problems society faces at this time will only be solved with the right balance of worldly and spiritual solutions. And mercy is an essential ingredient.

It's time to imagine a culture where mercy is embraced as the cultural norm. It's time to open our hearts to the mercy God yearns to fill us with. Are you willing to become an instrument of God's mercy?

OUR PERSONAL NEED FOR MERCY

Any culture that celebrates things that will destroy it is doomed. Our culture is celebrating and encouraging the catalog of human vice on an industrial scale, and any culture is made up of the people that participate in it.

We are in desperate need of mercy, and our need is much greater than we realize, as we will soon discover. Now imagine you need 100 grams of a medication each day to be healed and stay healthy, but you only take 5 grams each day. You will wonder each day why the medication is not working, but the reason is clear. You may be tempted to think the medication is useless, when in fact you just need a higher dose.

We need more mercy than we realize. Sometimes we don't realize how significant the gap is between who we are today and who God created us to be. At church on Sunday after the Gospel has been read, I often ask myself: "If I just lived this one Gospel reading 100 percent, how much would my life change?" The answer is the same every Sunday: radically. My life would change radically if I lived just one parable or one teaching from the Gospels 100 percent. Not a little bit. Radically.

What that tells me is that there is a gap between my life and the Gospel. And it's a big gap. It's an obvious gap. It's not even a close call. There is a gaping hole between my life and the life Jesus invites me to live in the Gospel—and I need God's mercy to help close that gap.

It's good to recognize the gap. Part of the problem, it seems, is that most of us think we are pretty good Christians. But compared to what? If we compare ourselves to what we see in the movies, you might be able to convince yourself you are virtually a saint. But is that a true measure of a Christian? I don't think so. Perhaps you look around at your friends and compare yourselves to them. Maybe compared to them you think you are an excellent Christian.

But when the young man came to Jesus and said, "Teacher, what must I do to inherit eternal life?" (Luke 18:18) Jesus didn't say, "Oh, just be better than the people around you."

Anyone can find a comparison to help them feel good about themselves. This charade assists us in deceiving ourselves in a thousand ways. This is the sin of comparison.

Some people may look at the gap between the life I am currently leading and the Gospel and judge me. They may be tempted to think, "He says he is a Christian, but he does this or that." They may be tempted to say, "He is a hypocrite." They would be right. I have no defense. I struggle every day to live the life Jesus invites us to. I am weak and broken. I have biases and prejudices. I am a sinner. But knowing I am a sinner is not the same as self-loathing. So, I do not give up, I press on, striving to be better and do better.

Despite this gap, I still consider myself a disciple of Jesus. Membership among the followers of Jesus Christ does not require perfection. But it does require us to strive to live the Gospel more fully each day. And that means opening ourselves up to His grace and mercy, and working diligently to close the gap.

THE FOUR MOVEMENTS OF MERCY

Mercy is a divine symphony composed of four transformative movements. These movements unfold in a way that mirrors our journey through life.

The First Movement: Becoming Aware of Your Need for Mercy

The first movement begins with an awakening—a recognition of your profound need for mercy. This awareness often arises from moments of failure, loss, or vulnerability when the illusion of self-sufficiency fades away. You see your flaws, limitations, and sins with clarity, and the weight of imperfection becomes undeniable. This realization is humbling, but it is also essential to our transformation. Becoming aware of your need for mercy is itself a great grace.

The Second Movement: Opening Your Heart to Mercy
The second movement invites you to receive what you cannot earn: God's unmerited mercy. This step requires vulnerability, trust, and an open heart. Experiencing mercy is unlike anything else. It is deeply personal, and yet, universally transformative. In this moment, God's love washes over you, revealing that you are cherished. Mercy convinces you that you are more than the worst thing you have ever done, more than everything and anything you have ever done. Mercy is no longer an abstract concept but a lived reality. It breaks the chains of guilt and shame, freeing you to see yourself as God sees you—loved and redeemable.

The Third Movement: Being Transformed by Mercy
The third movement is the most profound. Mercy does not merely comfort. It transforms. As it takes root in your heart, it begins to reshape your thoughts, desires, and actions. You are no longer defined by your past failures or limitations, but by the grace that now flows through you. Mercy softens the hard edges of bitterness and self-condemnation, filling you with compassion, humility, and gratitude. This inner transformation is a testimony to the power of God's love, which makes all things new.

The Fourth Movement: Becoming a Pilgrim of Mercy
The final movement is the crescendo—the point where mercy flows outward. Having received God's abundant mercy, and having been transformed by His mercy, you become a Pilgrim of Mercy, sharing it with all those who cross your path. You forgive

others as you have been forgiven, extend compassion to those in need, and embody kindness and hope. This isn't just a random act of kindness. It's a calling to participate in God's work of restoration.

These four movements aren't linear. They aren't one and done. It's a lifelong process, a recurring cycle. Each time we work our way through the cycle we grow in virtue and character. The journey for a Pilgrim of Mercy continues.

If you would like a deeper understanding of the four movements, I encourage you to find when and how they occurred in the lives of your favorite saints.

These four movements create a symphony of mercy that has the power to animate our lives, families, communities, and indeed, the whole world. This spiritual pilgrimage was designed to inspire you to explore and embrace these four movements. I hope over the next thirty-three days you are able to identify your need for mercy, open your heart to mercy, be transformed by mercy, and become a Pilgrim of Mercy.

WHAT IS CONSECRATION?

Consecration is to devote yourself to God and make yourself 100 percent available to carry out His will on this earth. It is an act of unconditional surrender to God. Through the act of consecration, we dedicate ourselves abundantly, wholeheartedly, and completely to the will of God, surrender our distractions and selfishness, and promise to faithfully respond to God's grace in our lives.

In the Book of Exodus, after the incident with the golden calf, Moses realized that the people had lost their way, and so he called them together and said, "Consecrate yourselves today to the Lord... that he may bestow upon you a blessing this day." (Exodus 32:29)

In the First Book of Chronicles, after God chose his son Solomon to lead, David gave everything he had over to God and the people of Israel. And then he asked, "Who else among you will contribute generously and consecrate themselves to the Lord this day?" (1 Chronicles 29:5)

In the Book of Joshua, God's chosen people entered the Promised Land after wandering in the desert for forty years. Joshua asked the priests to carry the Ark of the Covenant before the people and said, "Consecrate yourselves to the Lord, for tomorrow he will do wonders among you." (Joshua 3:5)

33 Days to Divine Mercy is a spiritual pilgrimage designed to lead you into a profound encounter with God's mercy.

THE INCREDIBLE JOURNEY BEFORE YOU

You are about to embark on an incredible journey. This isn't just another book. It is an invitation to participate in a sacred journey—a spiritual pilgrimage. It's a guide that will lead you to discover God's vast mercy... and it will change your life in the most marvelous of ways.

This consecration will take your spiritual life to new heights, but it will also energize the way you participate in relationships; ignite a new curiosity about yourself and others; transform the way you think about money and things; refocus your professional life; liberate you from many of your fears, doubts, and anxieties; make you aware of the hopes and dreams God has placed in your heart; and breathe new life into your appreciation for the genius of Catholicism.

Along the way you will meet many people who desperately need what you are holding in your hands right now. I hope you will share it with them. By sharing this consecration with them, you will become a Pilgrim of Mercy, preparing their hearts for Jesus to enter and transform them.

THE HISTORY OF DIVINE MERCY

The Divine Mercy devotion has gained popularity since Saint Faustina was canonized by Pope John Paul II in 2000. But it is important to understand that Divine Mercy is first and foremost a defining characteristic of God that people have been encountering throughout salvation history in a variety of ways.

Divine Mercy in the Old Testament
The concept of Divine Mercy is deeply rooted in the Old Testament. The Hebrew term *hesed* refers to God's steadfast love, covenantal faithfulness, and mercy.

Exodus 34:6-7: God reveals Himself to Moses as "merciful and gracious, slow to anger, abounding in steadfast love and faithfulness."

Psalm 136: A litany of God's mercy, with the refrain, "His mercy endures forever."

Hosea 6:6: "I desire mercy, not sacrifice."

God's mercy is shown through His forgiveness of Israel's sins, His deliverance of His people from Egypt, and His ongoing covenant despite their failings.

Prophets like Isaiah, Jeremiah, and Hosea emphasize God's desire for repentance and restoration rather than punishment, showcasing mercy as a hallmark of divine action.

The New Testament and the Catholic Church
In the New Testament, Jesus reveals the mercy of God through His teachings, miracles, and sacrifice. But even more importantly, through His Passion and Death, Jesus reveals Himself as mercy.

Just as we say, "God is love," (John 4:8) we can profess, Jesus is Mercy.

Mercy is a recurring theme in the parables of Jesus, perhaps none more poignant than the parable of the Prodigal Son (Luke 15:11-32) and the parable of the Good Samaritan. (Luke 10:25-37) Mercy was also central to the way Jesus encountered people. There are so many examples. The woman caught in adultery (John 8:1-11), the healing of the paralytic lowered through the roof (Mark 2:1-12), the healing of the blind man Bartimaeus (Mark 10:46-52), the Samaritan woman at the well (John 4:1-42), forgiving Peter after his denials (John 21:15-19), promising eternal life to the criminal on the Cross (Luke 23:39-43), and those words from the Cross that apply to us all, "Father, forgive them, for they know not what they do." (Luke 23:34)

The teachings of the Catholic Church have always emphasized mercy, and the sacraments are offered as a powerful encounter with God's mercy, particularly the Sacrament of Reconciliation.

The Church has also consistently taught that we have a responsibility to share God's mercy with others. This is uniquely manifested in the seven Corporal Works of Mercy and the seven Spiritual Works of Mercy, which we will explore during our thirty-three-day pilgrimage.

These Works of Mercy (both corporal and spiritual) are foundational to Catholic social teaching.

Mercy and the Sacred Heart Devotion

Saint Margaret Mary Alacoque (1647–1690) was a French Visitation nun who experienced visions of Jesus. During these visions, Jesus spoke to her about His Sacred Heart as a symbol of His love and mercy for humanity.

Jesus expressed His desire for humanity to draw closer to His heart, particularly through Eucharistic devotion and reparation for sins. This led Pope Pius IX to institute the Feast of the Sacred Heart on the Friday after the Feast of Corpus Christi.

The Sacred Heart Devotion led generations of Catholics to a deeper understanding of God's unconditional love and abundant mercy.

Saint Faustina Kowalska and the Divine Mercy Devotion

"Jesus, I trust in You." This phrase is at the heart of the Divine Mercy devotion promoted by Saint Faustina Kowalska (1905–1938), a Polish nun who received visions of Jesus. The central message of their encounters was His mercy. Jesus emphasized that His mercy is greater than all human sin and that trust in His mercy is essential for salvation.

The Divine Mercy devotion is made up of these five practices.

The Feast: Every year, on the Sunday after Easter, the Church celebrates Divine Mercy Sunday. This special feast was requested by Jesus Himself: "I desire that the Feast of Mercy be a refuge and shelter for all souls, and especially for poor sinners. On that day the very depths of My tender mercy are open... The soul that will go to Confession and receive Holy Communion shall obtain complete forgiveness of sins and punishment." You can celebrate Divine Mercy Sunday each year by attending Mass, going to Confession, and praying the Divine Mercy Chaplet.

The Image: When Jesus first appeared to Faustina, He was wearing white, with His right hand raised in a blessing. His left hand was touching His heart, where two rays flowed out. Jesus said: "Paint an image according to the pattern you see, with the signature: Jesus, I trust in You. I promise that the soul that will venerate this image will not perish... I desire that this image be venerated, first in your chapel, and [then] throughout the world."

With the help of her spiritual director, Faustina commissioned an artist named Eugeniusz Kazimirowski to paint the image as Jesus requested.

The Novena: The Divine Mercy Novena is a special prayer that asks Jesus to bless the world with His Divine Mercy. Jesus taught Faustina this special novena and said: "I will deny nothing to any soul whom you will bring to the fount of My mercy." You can pray the Divine Mercy Novena any time of year, but traditionally the Church prays it for nine days from Good Friday to Divine Mercy Sunday.

The Chaplet: Jesus taught Faustina to pray the Chaplet of Divine Mercy and made an amazing promise: "When [you] say this Chaplet in the presence of the dying, I will stand between My father and the dying person, not as the Just Judge but as the Merciful Savior." You can pray the Chaplet of Divine Mercy for any intention, but it is especially powerful to pray for people who will die on this day throughout the world.

The Hour of Mercy: Every day at three o'clock in the afternoon is a sacred moment of mercy. Jesus told Faustina: "As often as you hear the clock strike the third hour, immerse yourself completely in My mercy... In this hour you can obtain everything for yourself and for others for the asking; it was the hour of grace for the whole world—mercy triumphed over justice." You can celebrate the Hour of Mercy by setting an alarm on your phone and saying a short prayer, making a visit to a church, or praying the Chaplet of Divine Mercy.

The Catholic Church has a rich history of celebrating and sharing God's mercy with the people of every age. Every day the Catholic Church feeds more people, houses more people, clothes more people, educates more people, and visits more prisoners than any other group of people on planet earth. And we have been doing these things for a long time.

Divine Mercy is the infinite and eternal love and compassion God has for humanity. Our family, the biggest family in history—the Catholic Church—has been sharing that mercy with people for two thousand years.

The Catholic Church continues to bring God's mercy to the ends of the earth, and all Catholics are compelled to participate in that mission.

HOW TO USE THIS BOOK

Over the next thirty-three days you are going to take a spiritual pilgrimage. Some people go on pilgrimage to the Holy Land, Fatima, Lourdes, Santiago de Compostela or Rome. I hope you can join us one day on one of our amazing pilgrimages to these places. But this spiritual pilgrimage you can make in the comfort of your favorite chair. And yet, it will be the longest journey you ever make without moving an inch.

A pilgrimage is a sacred journey with a specific intention. Our journey will be an inner journey, and our specific intention is consecration to Divine Mercy.

This book is intended as a handbook for your spiritual pilgrimage. The readings, prayers, and other resources are arranged day-by-day and under a weekly theme. This is a time of preparation for the profound experience of consecration to Divine Mercy. The reflections are designed to be deeply spiritual and intensely practical.

This preparation will require about fifteen minutes each day. Here is a step-by-step guide to each day:

1. Find a quiet place.
2. Read the reflection.
3. Ponder the one idea that struck you most from the reading for a few minutes.

4. Pray the Divine Mercy Prayer.
5. Look for opportunities to adopt the virtue of the day amidst your daily activities.
6. Have a great day!

The journey will last thirty-three days. Four weeks and five days. Each week is arranged around a theme and designed to prepare you for your consecration on day thirty-three, but also to educate and inspire you about the extraordinary power of Divine Mercy.

Week One:	Divine Mercy and the Pilgrim
Week Two:	Divine Mercy and the Saints
Week Three:	The Corporal Works of Mercy
Week Four:	The Spiritual Works of Mercy
The Final Days:	Surrender

If you miss a day, don't get discouraged, and don't quit. Every evil force in the universe wants you to do that. You will feel the pull of those evil spirits at times. And the pull of those evil spirits will be tempting you to abandon this pilgrimage. Don't. See those temptations for what they are: proof that what you are doing is a powerful spiritual exercise that is going to bear abundant fruit in your life and for the world.

If you miss a day, or two days, or even five days, do not give in to discouragement. Discouragement doesn't come from God.

If you miss days, simply read the days you missed, and keep moving forward. You will be tempted to abandon this journey or tempted to go back and start again. Don't. This again is just the pull of evil spirits that do not want you to complete this consecration.

If you started praying the rosary and started over each time you got distracted, you would never finish a single rosary.

Stay the course. Don't give in to distraction or discouragement. No matter what, thirty-three days after you start: consecrate yourself to Jesus, the Divine Mercy. Day 33 lays out clearly how to complete the Act of Consecration.

LET THE PILGRIMAGE BEGIN

You are about to become a Pilgrim of Mercy.

Divine Mercy is our destination. Our goal is to have a deeply personal, utterly radical encounter with Divine Mercy. Along the way, we will learn about God's astounding mercy, open our hearts to receiving it, and discover practical ways to share it. But ultimately, this pilgrimage is about encountering Jesus and allowing Him to transform our hearts and minds.

Jesus knows we are broken. He knows our lives are a mess. He knows the struggles we have relating with each other. He knows we get overwhelmed. And yet, He stands before us, beckoning us to come to Him.

If we accept this invitation from Jesus our lives will forever be changed. He is waiting to heal you, forgive you, and remind you that you are enough. It's time to bring your mess to Jesus and open yourself up to His mercy.

The beautiful thing is mercy is contagious. So, as we encounter God's generous mercy, we have a growing desire to share His mercy with others.

A Pilgrim of Mercy journeys through life sharing kindness, compassion, forgiveness, and love.

We live in a world marked by division, judgment, and suffering. A Pilgrim of Mercy walks a different path—one illuminated by God's grace and guided by the call to bring mercy to others.

This journey is not confined to a single destination but unfolds in everyday encounters, where acts of mercy transform lives and relationships.

A Pilgrim of Mercy begins by recognizing their own need for God's forgiveness. This humility fosters empathy, making us more attuned to the struggles and wounds of others.

A Pilgrim of Mercy recognizes those who are burdened by guilt, pain, and regret. They do not walk with condemnation but with understanding, reminding others that our God is a God of second chances.

This pilgrimage requires courage and perseverance. It challenges societal norms that value retribution over reconciliation, and pride over humility. But a Pilgrim of Mercy stays the course, remembering that each act of mercy can have an unimaginable impact.

Over the next thirty-three days I will be praying and fasting for you. I pray this spiritual pilgrimage will be a profound and deeply mystical journey. May the Divine Mercy of Jesus Christ find a home deep in your soul and remain with you forever.

This is His invitation to you today: "Come to me, all you that are weary and are carrying heavy burdens, and I will give you rest." (Matthew 11:28)

And His message to you today is unmistakable. In a world where so many people feel unseen, unheard, and unworthy, Jesus generously proclaims: *I see you. I hear you. I know you. You are worthy. I am with you. I care. I am yours. You are Mine.*

Jesus wants to enter your heart in a new way. But the door to your heart can only be opened from the inside. It has no handle on the outside. And so, the words from the Book of Revelation take on a deeply personal meaning for us today: "Behold, I stand at the door knocking." (Revelation 3:20)

Will you open the door of your heart?

Trust. Surrender. Believe. Receive.

Matthew Kelly

DAY 1
WHAT IS MERCY?

"Goodness and mercy will follow me all the days of my life."
Psalm 23:6

There are words we use all the time, hear all the time, and yet, we aren't always clear about their meaning. What is mercy? The world's definition of mercy is "compassion or forgiveness shown toward someone whom it is within one's power to punish or harm."

But the mercy of God is much more than an act of pardon or the cancellation of punishment. It is more dynamic than the passivity of looking the other way. It is intimate and deeply personal.

And so, we ask again, what is mercy? Mercy is love reaching out to misery. Love reaching out to misery. When we need God's mercy, we are miserable—the two go hand in hand.

We may be aware of our misery, or we may be oblivious to it. Sometimes it is misery that we have caused ourselves, sometimes we are the victims of misery someone else has caused, and sometimes our misery is caused by the seemingly random, inexplicable accidents, disasters, and tragedies of life.

Just know this: The next time you are miserable, God is reaching out to you. And that reaching out is mercy—love reaching out to misery.

And just as God reaches out to us with His love in the midst of our misery, we are called to lovingly reach out to others in their misery. We are called to become Pilgrims of Mercy.

I have witnessed people extend extraordinary mercy to others in the most ordinary ways: a touch, a smile, a helping hand. I have also seen human beings bestow astounding mercy on other human beings. How is that possible? Made in the image of God, we are capable of mercy. It is a divine attribute and a human capability.

Spend one minute meditating on Jesus' suffering on the Cross and then imagine how vast God's mercy must be. Imagine yourself immersed in His mercy. Ask Him to bathe you in His mercy.

God's mercy is greater than any mistake you can make. God's mercy will liberate you from the worst moments in your past, and His mercy is the key to the best moments in your future.

Saint Augustine of Hippo observed, "God's mercy is so great that you may sooner drain the sea of its water, or deprive the sun of its light, than diminish the great mercy of God."

Our need for God's mercy is vast, but His mercy is boundless. He is always reaching out to us mercifully, as a loving Father, hoping to save us from the next misery we are creating for ourselves.

Mercy is love reaching out to misery. What misery do you need God to reach out to and soothe today?

Trust. Surrender. Believe. Receive.

LESSON

What is mercy? Mercy is love reaching out to misery. Anytime you are miserable, God is reaching out to you. When we reach out to others in their misery we are extending God's mercy to them. We are Pilgrims of Mercy.

VIRTUE OF THE DAY

Faith: The virtue of faith is a gift. You can work hard to develop many virtues, but with faith, we ask: "Lord, increase my faith." Ask dozens of times each day. And as your faith grows, you will see more and more miracles, until finally, you will realize everything is a miracle.

DIVINE MERCY PRAYER

Eternal God, in whom mercy is endless and the treasury of compassion inexhaustible, look kindly upon us and increase Your mercy in us, that in difficult moments we might not despair nor become despondent, but with great confidence submit ourselves to Your holy will, which is Love and Mercy itself. Amen.

DAY 2
WHO IS MERCY?

"Goodness and mercy will follow me all the days of my life."
Psalm 23:6

When we are trying to understand something, it is natural for us to ask: What is that? But in the case of divine attributes, we get a more complete understanding by asking: Who is that?

What is mercy? was yesterday's question. And the answer: Mercy is love reaching out to misery. Today's question: *Who is mercy?* And the answer: God—and more specifically, Jesus.

"Jesus Christ is the face of the Father's mercy," Pope Francis reminds us. Pope John Paul II observed, "In Christ and through Christ, God becomes especially visible in His mercy... He Himself in a certain sense is mercy."

Jesus is Mercy.

Jesus is the manifestation of God's redemptive love. He is God's mercy manifested for men, women, and children to experience and receive. And His mercy fills us with joy.

This mercy is essential if we are to learn to love each other again. There is no love without mercy and forgiveness. Without mercy and forgiveness any relationship will fail. Human relationships simply cannot survive without mercy and forgiveness.

He came to teach us how to love. He taught us to love one another as He has loved us. Mercy is love reaching out to misery. Who would describe you as merciful? Jesus is Mercy. Do your actions remind others of Jesus?

If your answers to these questions look anything like my answers, we've got work to do. The good news is everything good and noble on this planet, along with all the angels and saints in Heaven, are on our side.

When I was fifteen, I was challenged to read the four Gospels for fifteen minutes a day, over and over again for a year. Just the Gospels. I learned so much about Jesus that year. It also gave me a great love of these books in the Bible.

As Catholics, we experience the Bible so many times throughout the course of our lives. The readings at Mass on Sunday, attending weddings and baptisms, funerals and feast days, all expose us to God's message to humanity in the Scriptures.

So, I am always looking for new and fresh ways to experience the Scriptures. Our journey together over these thirty-three days provides a very specific opportunity to experience the Gospels in a new way.

Over the next few days, take fifteen minutes, pick up your Bible, find a quiet place, get comfortable, take a deep breath, and start reading the Gospel of Matthew. Every time you read the name of Jesus, replace it with mercy, and listen to what that phrase or passage says to you. I think you will find it to be a profound and powerful experience.

Here is a sampling of references to Jesus from the beginning of the Gospel of Matthew:

"An account of the genealogy of Mercy (Jesus) the Messiah the son of David the son of Abraham." (Matthew 1:1)

An account of the genealogy of Mercy. Wow! How beautiful is that? The Messiah brings redemption and salvation to humanity. Redemption and salvation are by their very nature acts of astounding mercy.

"... and Jacob the father of Joseph the husband of Mary, of whom Mercy (Jesus) was born who is called the Messiah." (Matthew 1: 16)

Mother of Mercy is one of the Church's official names for Mary because of her unique role in salvation history. Mary's role as mother makes her the embodiment of God's loving compassion toward humanity. Jesus is Mercy Incarnate.

"Joseph, son of David, do not be afraid to take Mary as your wife, for the child conceived in her is from the Holy Spirit. She will bear a son, and you are to name him Mercy (Jesus), for he will save his people from their sins." (Matthew 1: 20-21)

Mercy has saved us from our sins. Forgiveness is a core Christian belief. Forgiveness and salvation go hand in hand. Do you need to forgive somebody? I know I do. I am really struggling to forgive a couple of people in my life right now and this is a direct, in-my-face reminder of that. But maybe your need is to be forgiven, or accept forgiveness? And perhaps you need to forgive yourself?

"From that time Mercy (Jesus) began to proclaim, 'Repent, for the kingdom of heaven has come near.'" (Matthew 4:17)

It is merciful to invite people to turn back to God. Repentance unlocks mercy. It opens the door of our hearts to mercy. Mercy is always an invitation to a better life, in large ways and small ways. God's mercy stirs the human heart, nudging it toward repentance. Mercy originates with God. Full of compassion, He reaches out to us freely offering forgiveness.

Jesus is Mercy. Jesus is Divine Mercy. This pilgrimage—this thirty-three-day journey—is an invitation to get to know Jesus in new ways. There is a profound connection between healing and mercy. The people I encounter each day are all in need of healing. I need healing. The type of healing we need may be different—physical, emotional, intellectual, psychological, relational, spiritual—but there is one source of healing for us all: Jesus Christ, the Divine Mercy.

He wants to heal us. He wants to teach us how to love again. He wants to bathe us in His mercy, convince us of His mercy, fill us with His mercy, and send us out into the world as Pilgrims of Mercy.

Trust. Surrender. Believe. Receive.

LESSON

Jesus is Mercy. Jesus is the manifestation of God's redemptive love. He is God's mercy manifested for men, women, and children to experience and receive. And His mercy fills us with joy.

VIRTUE OF THE DAY

Joy: The virtue of joy is a long-lasting state beyond happiness that is not dependent on external circumstances to be sustained. It is possible to be suffering and experience joy at the same time. The flames of joy can be fanned in our hearts with gratitude and service to others. Joy is the fruit of appreciation.

DIVINE MERCY PRAYER

Eternal God, in whom mercy is endless and the treasury of compassion inexhaustible, look kindly upon us and increase Your mercy in us, that in difficult moments we might not despair nor become despondent, but with great confidence submit ourselves to Your holy will, which is Love and Mercy itself.

We would love to send you a FREE Companion Journal—A Day-by-Day Guide to Your Spiritual Journey. Scan the QR code or visit www.PilgrimsofMercy.com/2 to view your special offer!

DAY 3
A NEW BEGINNING

"Goodness and mercy will follow me all the days of my life."
Psalm 23:6

I love Mondays because each Monday is a new beginning—a fresh start! God gives us Mondays, New Year's Day, birthdays, and every single one represents a new blessing and a new beginning. New beginnings are a beautiful gift.

"It's just another day," some people say. They are right and they are wrong. We get to decide. If you want it to be just another random day, that's your choice. If you want it to be the first day of something new and beautiful, that's your choice too.

One of the things I love about our faith is that our God is a God of second chances, fresh starts, and new beginnings.

This consecration to Divine Mercy is a new beginning. New beginnings and second chances are full of hope and possibilities. Christianity is about new beginnings. Our God is a God of second, third, fourth, fifth, and seventy-seventh chances. God loves new beginnings.

Jesus is the ultimate new beginning. Divine Mercy is the ultimate second chance. Jesus invites us to leave behind the old and step into the new. This is not merely a call to change our circumstances but to transform our hearts, our minds, and our souls.

What is Jesus inviting you to leave behind?

Too often, we allow the weight of our past mistakes to prevent us from living the life God is calling us to live today. It's so easy to get trapped in repetitive thought cycles that focus on our past mistakes and the guilt, shame, and regret that came from them. These thought patterns are exhausting. Divine Mercy wants to liberate you from your obsessive thoughts about your past. You are not the worst thing you have done, and Divine Mercy is greater than every poor choice you have ever made.

"Father, forgive them, for they know not what they do." (Luke 23:34) These were not empty words. They are a declaration of His compassion and mercy.

"I have come that they may have life, and have it to the fullest." (John 10:10) These were not empty words either. They are a testament to His power to make all things new.

Are you ready for a new beginning? Throughout His life Jesus was constantly offering people second chances and new beginnings. Tax collectors, adulterers, lepers, prostitutes and the possessed, the disciples and the thief on the cross. His message was clear: Everyone deserves a new beginning.

Peter is a perfect example. One of Jesus' first disciples, Peter loved Jesus deeply. But in Jesus' darkest hour, Peter denied Him three times. Imagine the shame and self-loathing Peter must have felt. And yet, after His Resurrection Jesus didn't cast Peter aside, He drew him nearer than ever. He knew Peter loved Him and ultimately would appoint Peter as the first pope.

Jesus was telling Peter that his past mistakes did not define his future, and Jesus is telling you the same thing today. He will not allow your past mistakes to define your future. This is central to Christianity: the belief that we are not defined by our worst moments.

Jesus gives us the grace to start again. But to embrace our new beginning, we need to release our grip on the things that no longer serve us: regret, bitterness, pride, fear, and doubt.

But letting go isn't easy. It requires trust—trust in God's plan and trust in His timing. Proverbs encourages us, "Trust in the Lord with all your heart." (Proverbs 3:5-6) When we place our trust in God, we can step into the unknown with confidence, knowing that He is with us every step of the way.

This trust is at the heart of Divine Mercy.

Allow me to share two practical ways to nurture and cultivate trust within your soul.

The first is to pray. "Jesus, I trust in You." Pray this short prayer over and over again as we make our pilgrimage together. When you are uncertain and afraid, pray: "Jesus, I trust in You." When you are hopeful about your new beginning, pray: "Jesus, I trust in You." When you feel overwhelmed and life seems chaotic, pray: "Jesus, I trust in You."

Become trustworthy. We struggle to trust God because we aren't completely trustworthy ourselves. Truth brings order to our lives. Truth is the foundation of integrity. Truth is a path to growth. Tell the truth and seek the truth. Your ability to trust God will expand the more trustworthy you become yourself.

Now, what's holding you back from your new beginning? What burden do you need to lay at the foot of the Cross? Jesus is waiting with open arms, ready to walk with you into a future filled with hope and promise. The question is not whether He can transform your life but whether you will let Him. Say yes to Him today and He will turn the page to a new chapter in your life.

It is never too late for a fresh start.

"Ask and it will be given to you; search and you will find; knock, and the door will be opened for you." (Matthew 7:7)

Ask God to grant you a new beginning today.

Trust. Surrender. Believe. Receive.

LESSON

Our God is a God of second chances, fresh starts, and new beginnings. Throughout His life Jesus was constantly offering people second chances and new beginnings. Nothing you have done excludes you. His message was clear: Everyone deserves a new beginning.

VIRTUE OF THE DAY

Determination: The virtue of determination allows us to focus on a task and see it through to completion. Just keep moving in the direction of your goal or destination. Determination is taking the next step, no matter how small that step may be.

DIVINE MERCY PRAYER

Eternal God, in whom mercy is endless and the treasury of compassion inexhaustible, look kindly upon us and increase Your mercy in us, that in difficult moments we might not despair nor become despondent, but with great confidence submit ourselves to Your holy will, which is Love and Mercy itself.

DAY 4
AN AUTHENTIC SENSE OF SELF

"Goodness and mercy will follow me all the days of my life."
Psalm 23:6

When we were starting our family, Meggie and I talked a lot about how we wanted to raise our children and some of the outcomes that were important to us. One of our goals has always been to raise children who love learning. We decided that fostering a love of learning was more important than grades, because we believe if they love learning, they will look for ways to learn every day for the rest of their lives.

More important than a love of learning, we decided we wanted to help our children develop a strong sense of self while they were very young. We knew the world would try to rob them of their very selves, because that is what our culture is doing to people, and we wanted to try to help them build a cultural defense system. And at the core of this we believed was a strong sense of self.

In his poem, "Second Coming," William Butler Yeats wrote,

*"The falcon cannot hear the falconer;
Things fall apart; the centre cannot hold."*
The message is clear. Things fall apart when we can't hear the voice of God in our lives. Separated from God, the center of our lives cannot hold, and chaos and confusion take over.

One of the most toxic and tragic developments in our culture since the turn of the new millennium has been the focus on identity politics. Identity politics refers to a political approach where individuals or groups advocate for policies, rights, and representation based on shared aspects of their identity, such as race, gender, sexual orientation, ethnicity, religion, or other social characteristics. This approach is bound to create division, undermine merit, promote victimhood, and denies individuality by reducing people to their group identities.

The great confusion of our age surrounds identity. This has led to identity wars that fail to recognize the most important aspect of our identity. The primary aspect of a person's identity isn't their age, race, body size, immigration status, disability, religion, gender, sexual orientation, or socio-economic class. And the primary aspect of a person's identity isn't different from one person to the next, it is the same for us all: We are children of God.

When we try to place something else at the core of our identity, the result will always be pain and confusion.

I identify as a child of God.

I am Australian by birth, I am an American citizen, I am fifty-one years old, I am a husband and a father, I am a white male, I am an author, I am a Christian, I am a Catholic, and there are many more aspects to my identity, but they are all secondary to my identity as a child of God.

This is what binds us all together. This is what makes us one. This will be the source of our unity when we acknowledge, respect, and celebrate it; and it will be the source of our division when we deny it or deprioritize it.

Our culture is full of identity confusion. As parents we are constantly vigilant regarding the identity our children are taking on as a result of daily interaction with other people and the culture. I want my children to know that they are children of a Great King. I made a poster to hang in my daughter's room that reads:

"I am the daughter of a Great King. He is my Father and my God. The world may praise me or criticize me. It matters not. He is with me, always at my side, guiding and protecting me. I do not fear because I am His."

In the boys' room, there is the same poster with just a couple of changes: "I am the son of a Great King..."

Our identity comes from God. When we turn our backs on God or cast Him aside, our lives become adrift. Our center cannot hold, and we become lost and confused.

Today we have people saying, "I identify as this..." or "I identify as that..." but this is an aberration. Our primary identity is as children of God.

We are children of God. I identify as a child of God. I want my children to draw their sense of self from this great truth.

One of the plagues of our age is unworthiness. So many people think they are not enough. Societal expectations, endless comparisons driven by social media, an explosion of envy, excessive criticism and neglect in childhood, perfectionism, and unrealistic standards all leave people feeling unloved, unworthy, inherently flawed, inadequate, and unlovable.

The more we understand and believe we are the sons and daughters of a Great King, the less we are likely to experience these feelings of inadequacy. If we believed with our whole hearts that we are children of God, and therefore of infinite value, we wouldn't believe these things about ourselves.

Too many of us have a very poor sense of self. God wants to repair and restore our sense of self.

A clear sense of self empowers you to live authentically. You embrace your strengths and acknowledge your limitations without being defined by them. This self-awareness fosters confidence and resilience, enabling you to endure challenges and uncertainties. It also allows you to develop fulfilling relationships by setting and maintaining healthy boundaries. A strong sense of self guides you to make decisions that align with your values and beliefs, which ensures you invest your energy in what truly matters.

The wisdom of Divine Mercy helps us to develop an authentic sense of self by giving us the courage to face all that is true about ourselves and liberating us from all that is false.

Saint Teresa of Ávila wrote, "Humility is truth." This simple statement reflects a profound understanding. Humility isn't about thinking less of ourselves, putting ourselves down, or denying our inherent worth. It's about acknowledging reality. We are children of God who are capable of amazing things. We are finite, fallible, and sinful. And we are completely and utterly dependent on God who is the source of life and everything good. "For in Him we live and move and have our being." (Acts 17:28) This is reality and the more our sense of self is grounded in these truths, the more authentic our sense of self will be.

But let there be no confusion about who you are: You are a child of God.

If we could truly comprehend the concept that God is *Our Father*, if we could internalize this truth, we would never get past *Our Father* in the prayer. Just whispering the words *Our Father* would leave us stupefied.

You are the son or daughter of a Great King.

Trust. Surrender. Believe. Receive.

LESSON
You are the son or daughter of a Great King. He is your Father and your God. The world may praise you or criticize you. It matters not. He is with you, always at your side, guiding and protecting you. You do not fear because you are His. You were created in the image of God. You are enough.

VIRTUE OF THE DAY
Trust: The virtue of trust is in many ways an acknowledgment of the reality that God is in control. It is also a belief that God has a plan for our lives and will provide for us in that plan. One of the most practical ways to grow in the virtue of trust is to become more trustworthy. Trust determines how we participate in relationships. Who we trust reveals our character. The gift of trust is a tranquil soul.

DIVINE MERCY PRAYER
Eternal God, in whom mercy is endless and the treasury of compassion inexhaustible, look kindly upon us and increase Your mercy in us, that in difficult moments we might not despair nor become despondent, but with great confidence submit ourselves to Your holy will, which is Love and Mercy itself.

DAY 5
MERCY ISN'T EARNED

"Goodness and mercy will follow me all the days of my life."
Psalm 23:6

Once upon a time there was a priest who sat in the confessional in his church every day. People would come from all over to confess and receive his spiritual counsel.

At about the same time each day, he would hear some loud clanging noises at the back of the church. A few minutes would pass and then he would hear the clanging again. The priest was always curious about this noise.

One morning he exited the confessional just as the second clang was ringing out. Hurrying toward the back of the church, he found one of the local farmers leaving the church with his tools.

"Do you come here every morning?" the priest asked the farmer.

"Yes, Father," he replied.

"What do you do here?"

"I just sit a little and pray," the simple farmer replied.

"How do you pray?"

The farmer was a simple man and a little embarrassed by the priest's inquiry. Bowing his head, he said, "I look at the good God, and the good God looks at me."

Simple and beautiful. Practical and profound.

The priest was the Curé of Ars—Saint John Vianney. Like so many of the central figures in the Gospels, we don't know who the farmer was or how the rest of his life unfolded, but his simple wisdom about prayer lives on.

"I look at the good God, and the good God looks at me."

Our culture has a strong bias toward action. It is the fruit of our obsession with productivity. Together, our bias toward action and our obsession with productivity have eradicated any deeply rooted spirituality from most people's lives.

A man sitting quietly in church for an hour appears to be doing nothing, and when he is finished, he has nothing to show for his efforts. To the naked eye he appears to have accomplished nothing. Our culture believes this is a waste of time, but nothing could be further from the truth.

Mercy isn't earned. This is the essential dilemma we face as modern Christians when it comes to mercy. It isn't something you can earn. Not even with virtue. It is given. Freely. Completely. Mercy is bestowed on beggars.

Divine Mercy is the intervention our lives need, and the intervention our world needs.

Visit your local parish today and sit there quietly for a few minutes. You don't have to do anything. You don't have to say anything. Just sit there in the presence of the good God and allow Him to pour His infinite mercy into your soul.

Saint John Vianney, pray for us!

Trust. Surrender. Believe. Receive.

LESSON

Sometimes the hardest thing to do is nothing. For all our accomplishments and success, what we really need is grace and mercy, and they cannot be bought, earned, or won. This means there is nothing you can do to make God love you, and it means that you don't have to do anything to make God love you. All that is left is to learn to receive graciously that which we don't deserve but can't live without.

VIRTUE OF THE DAY

Receptivity: The virtue of receptivity involves opening our hearts, minds, bodies, and souls completely to God and allowing Him to work unimpeded on our souls and in our lives.

DIVINE MERCY PRAYER

Eternal God, in whom mercy is endless and the treasury of compassion inexhaustible, look kindly upon us and increase Your mercy in us, that in difficult moments we might not despair nor become despondent, but with great confidence submit ourselves to Your holy will, which is Love and Mercy itself.

Enhance your journey with daily videos from Matthew Kelly and other inspiring Catholic speakers! Scan the QR code or visit **www.PilgrimsofMercy.com/3** to view your special offer!

DAY 6
GENTLE KINDNESS

"Goodness and mercy will follow me all the days of my life."
Psalm 23:6

Silence gives birth to gratitude, and gratitude gives birth to gentle kindness.

It was by sitting alone in the presence of God in quiet empty churches that the Lord touched my life deeply. Out of the silence came a profound gratitude.

The virtue of gratitude is simply about recognizing the good that is already yours. Practicing gratitude sensitizes us to all the blessings God has bestowed upon us. It is easy to overlook all the good in our lives and focus on what is frustrating or lacking.

Sitting in the classroom of silence fills our hearts with gratitude. Sit still and quiet and let your heart and mind fill with grateful prayers to God.

I think about John Newton and the deep life of prayer that produced *Amazing Grace* and something stirs at the very core of my being. My soul yearns for a deeper connection with the Divine. And yet, I know that desire to pray itself is a gift, a grace, a tender mercy.

From this deep connection with God flows His abundant mercy and our souls are flooded with gratitude. And this mercy and gratitude transforms the way we relate with every person that crosses our paths. It fosters gentle kindness.

This gentle kindness is a blend of benevolence, compassion, love, mercy, and generosity. Rooted in the belief that all human beings are created in the image of God, gentle kindness goes beyond simple acts of kindness, calling us to mirror God's boundless mercy in our relations with each other. It is rooted in the Gospel teaching that whatever we do for another person, any other person, we do for Jesus.

The following passage is central to our pilgrimage with Divine Mercy. So, though you have heard it many times before, I encourage you to slow your spirit to reflect on it like never before.

"Then the King will say to those at his right hand, 'Come, O blessed of my Father, inherit the kingdom prepared for you from the foundation of the world; for I was hungry and you gave me food, I was thirsty and you gave me drink, I was a stranger and you welcomed me, I was naked and you clothed me, I was sick and you visited me, I was in prison and you came to me.' Then the righteous will answer him, 'Lord, when did we see thee hungry and feed thee, or thirsty and give thee drink? And when did we see thee a stranger and welcome thee, or naked and clothe thee? And when did we see thee sick or in prison and visit thee?' And the King will answer them, 'Truly, I say to you, as you did it to one of the least of these my brethren, you did it to me.' Then he will say to those at his left hand, 'Depart from me, you cursed, into the eternal fire prepared for the devil and his angels; for I was hungry and you gave me no food, I was thirsty and you gave me no drink, I was a stranger and you did not welcome me, naked and you did not clothe me, sick and in prison and you did not visit me.' Then they also will answer, 'Lord, when did we see thee hungry or thirsty or a stranger or naked or sick or in prison, and did not minister to thee?' Then he will answer them, 'Truly, I say to you, as you did it not to one of the least of these, you did it not to me.' And they will go away into eternal punishment, but the righteous into eternal life." (Matthew 25:34-46)

Serving others creates a profound connection between human beings and God. The more we experience God's gentle kindness the more we yearn to share it with others. And how do we foster this gentle kindness? Here is a handful of meditations I use throughout the day to put myself in a heartset to treat others with gentle kindness:

Assume each person you meet has just been told they are dying of cancer.

Imagine the person in front of you has just learned that the person they love most in this world has died.

Think of the person in front of you as someone who feels completely unseen, unheard, and unloved.

Imagine the person before you is silently battling overwhelming anxiety or depression.

Envision this person mourning the loss of a lifelong dream.

Assume the person you are with is silently struggling with chronic pain.

Would the world be a better place if we were all just a little more gentle, patient, kind, generous, thoughtful, and merciful? Let's allow God's mercy to flow through us and make it so.

Be gentle and kind with each other. These active meditations throughout the day will lead you to treat people differently. They will lead you to treat them with gentle kindness.

Kindness and gentleness—such simple things, but pure expressions of Divine Mercy. A Pilgrim of Mercy looks for opportunities to serve others with gentle kindness.

Trust. Surrender. Believe. Receive.

LESSON

Gentle kindness is a blend of benevolence, compassion, love, mercy, and generosity. Make love of God and love of neighbor the axis around which your life revolves. Walk the path of gentle kindness, constantly looking for opportunities to spend time with God and do good for others.

VIRTUE OF THE DAY

Gentleness: Far from being a sign of weakness, the virtue of gentleness is a sign of moral strength. It fosters harmony in relationships and builds trust. Gentleness combines self-control, compassion, and humility in our everyday interactions with other people.

DIVINE MERCY PRAYER

Eternal God, in whom mercy is endless and the treasury of compassion inexhaustible, look kindly upon us and increase Your mercy in us, that in difficult moments we might not despair nor become despondent, but with great confidence submit ourselves to Your holy will, which is Love and Mercy itself.

DAY 7
HUMILITY, HUMILITY, HUMILITY

"Goodness and mercy will follow me all the days of my life."
Psalm 23:6

The young seminarian was so excited. His new spiritual director was a living saint. Everyone spoke about him with hushed reverence. Some described him as a great saint, others told stories of how he had helped them discern difficult decisions, and there were some that whispered that he had the gift of reading souls.

Arriving in the old priest's study for his first spiritual direction session, the young man was giddy with excitement. Walking into the room, he found the old man sitting in his reader chair with his eyes closed. Sitting down, the seminarian wondered if his new spiritual director was asleep.

Five minutes passed and nothing happened. Ten minutes passed. Fifteen minutes. The young man decided that the old priest was in fact asleep, and stood up to leave, but in that moment the priest said, "Do you have a Bible with you?"

The young man felt foolish. He didn't. "I don't," he replied anxiously.

"There is one on the third shelf," the priest said.

Getting up, the seminarian walked over to the bookshelf. There was indeed a Bible on the third shelf, but there were about fifteen different Bibles. The whole shelf was full of Bibles.

"Which one?" he asked the old priest.

"You choose," was the reply.

The young seminarian chose a Bible and returned to his chair. As he passed the priest, he noticed his eyes were still closed.

"Good choice," the priest said.

How does he know without opening his eyes? the young man wondered to himself.

"Open your Bible to 1 John 1:9 and read it aloud for us to reflect upon," the priest instructed his new student.

"If we confess our sins, he is faithful and just, and will forgive our sins and cleanse us from all unrighteousness."

The young man and the old man sat in silence again, but a few moments later, the old priest, eyes closed still, began to speak, "When I was seven years old, I stole a candy bar from the corner store. . . " He continued to confess the sins of his life, in chronological order, for the next ten minutes.

The young seminarian sat there with his mouth wide open in shocked disbelief. He couldn't believe this man was confessing his sins to him, and he couldn't believe some of the sins this supposed living-saint had amassed over his life.

When the priest had finished confessing his sins to the seminarian he sat quietly for a few minutes. "Now you can decide if you still want me to be your spiritual director. If you do, I will see you at the same time next week, if you don't, I understand."

The seminarian stood to return the Bible to the bookshelf before leaving. "That's yours to keep. A gift from me," the priest said just as he was about to place it back on the shelf. "I love that Bible," he continued. "My father gave it to me on my first day of high school."

"I couldn't. . . " the seminarian began to say, but the priest raised his hand to silence his objection. Eyes still closed he replied, "Learning to receive graciously is an important lesson in the spiritual life."

The young man was speechless. He went straight to the chapel to reflect on this experience.

The old priest had seen right through him. He had indeed read his soul. The priest knew the seminarian had placed him high upon a massive pedestal, and in just a few minutes he had torn that pedestal down into a crumbling heap.

"Humility," the seminarian whispered to himself in the empty chapel. "Humility," he whispered again. "Humility," he whispered a third time. He sat in the chapel for over two hours reflecting on that one word, meditating on what it meant to him at the beginning of his journey toward priesthood.

Humility. "It was pride that changed angels into devils; it is humility that makes men as angels," Saint Augustine observed. And C.S. Lewis wrote, "As long as you are proud, you cannot know God. A proud man is always looking down on things and people; and, of course, as long as you are looking down, you cannot see something that is above you."

To walk humbly with God. That is the mandate placed before us in Micah 6:8, "He has shown you, O man, what is good. And what does the Lord require of you? To live justly, love tenderly, and to walk humbly with your God."

Our culture advocates incessant self-promotion, the flaunting of our material possession, and shameless boasting of worldly success. The fruits of these behaviors are pride, vanity, an inflated but empty sense of self, and a distorted view of what matters most. Humility in this environment is massively counter-cultural.

Cultivating humility in this cultural climate requires a conscious effort to shift our focus from self-centeredness to love of God and neighbor. One very practical way to foster a growing humility is to thank God specifically for a litany of things. Entitlement is a tell-tale sign of pride, and gratitude banishes entitlement. And one very practical litmus test of humility is to observe whether we are more interested in spiritual growth or external validation.

God wants to fill us with His mercy. Humility is the door through which God's mercy flows into our souls.

Trust. Surrender. Believe. Receive.

LESSON

God wants to fill us with His mercy. Humility is the door through which God's mercy flows into our souls, but our culture is obsessed with prideful self-promotion. Pride separates us from God. Ask yourself throughout the day: Am I walking humbly with my God?

VIRTUE OF THE DAY

Humility: The battle between humility and pride is central to the spiritual life. Pride contaminates anything that is good, destroys relationships, and blinds us to what is good, true, right, and just. It is the source of all moral evil. Jesus invites us to a life of humility because He is supremely interested in our happiness.

DIVINE MERCY PRAYER

Eternal God, in whom mercy is endless and the treasury of compassion inexhaustible, look kindly upon us and increase Your mercy in us, that in difficult moments we might not despair nor

become despondent, but with great confidence submit ourselves to Your holy will, which is Love and Mercy itself.

DAY 8
FAUSTINA: MERCY IS STRONGER THAN OUR MISERY

"Approach the throne of grace with boldness, so that we may receive mercy and find grace to help in time of need." Hebrews 4:16

Do you believe God has a plan for your life?

It's easy to see God's plan when we look at the lives of the saints. We have the benefit of hindsight. We know how their stories end. But it wasn't easy for them to see God's plan while their lives were unfolding. Their very human hearts were like your very human heart, and they yearned for happiness just as you do.

So how do you find happiness? The saints and mystics of every age came to understand one particular truth: Only God can make us happy. That's why one of the great quests of the spiritual life is to align our desires with God's desire. To want what God wants is wisdom. But it's not easy. Even the great patron saint of Divine Mercy, Sister Faustina Kowalska, struggled to discover God's great plan for her life.

As a teenager, Faustina dreamed of becoming a nun, but her parents refused to support her vocation. Then, at the age of nineteen, her path finally came into focus. While attending a local dance with her sister, she was dancing with a young man when Jesus appeared to her in a vision. He was wounded, bleeding, and asked her, "How long will you keep putting Me off?" Faustina left the dance and rushed to a nearby cathedral. Kneeling before the tabernacle, she begged Jesus to reveal His plan. She heard His voice clearly: *Go to Warsaw and join a convent there.*

You might assume that your life would be easier if Jesus would appear to you and tell you exactly what to do, but that wasn't the case for Faustina. When she arrived in Warsaw, she faced rejection after rejection. The convents all had their reasons for saying no: She was too old, too young, too poor, too uneducated. Finally, the Sisters of Our Lady of Mercy gave Faustina hope, telling her that she wasn't ready now, but she should return in a year. Faustina was deeply saddened by this delay, but as she worked and prayed, she continued to trust God's plan, wholeheartedly.

Years passed, Faustina entered the convent, and she settled into her vocation as a nun. But God's plan was just beginning. On February 22, 1931, Faustina was praying in her convent when Jesus appeared to her again. He was dressed in white with His right hand raised in a blessing. His left hand was on His heart, out of which flowed two brilliant rays, one red and one white.

In time this would become the legendary Divine Mercy image.

Jesus appeared to Faustina many times to teach her about His Divine Mercy and He asked Faustina to share it with the world. But even with her mission in hand, Faustina felt like everything was working against her.

She faced innumerable challenges that would have stopped most people in their tracks: People called her a liar; her superiors tried to stop her efforts; and she even came down with a deadly case of tuberculosis that would take her life at the young age of thirty-three.

These trials caused all sorts of doubts in Sister Faustina. At different points she thought to herself, *I'm not qualified. I'm not the right person for this.* But despite all of these moments when it looked like God's plan for her life was stalling, delayed, or even non-existent, Faustina trusted that God had a plan. As she trusted, that plan unfolded and so did an important truth: What God had planned for her was greater than what she could have wanted for herself.

God didn't just have a plan for Faustina—He had a plan to share His Divine Mercy with the entire world through her. A beautiful plan. A plan that we all fit into. If you learn nothing else from Faustina's story, learn this: Jesus has a wonderful plan for you and His mercy will help you overcome the doubts and obstacles you encounter along the way.

Jesus wanted Sister Faustina to experience His mercy and then share it with the world. Now Jesus wants you to experience His Divine Mercy and bring that mercy into the world, to share with your family, in the workplace, at school, and with the people who cross your path as you make your way through life. But here's the key: Trust that Jesus has a plan for you, no matter what.

Trusting God may seem overwhelming in a world where so many things go wrong so much of the time. But I will share with you the secret to allow trust to build in your heart: Place your trust in Him for today, and then wake up tomorrow and do the same thing.

Faustina never could have imagined what Jesus would do in her and through her, during her life and beyond. Trust that He will work through you for goodness. He will not disappoint you.

God reveals His plans little by little. Discovering His plan is an unfolding process that takes time, continuous effort, and above all, trust. So, begin today. Find a quiet place where you can be alone with God, allow the silence to settle your heart and mind, and ask God to reveal His will, not for the rest of your life, but for some situation you are dealing with right now.

A pilgrim's trust grows along the way. Allow your trust to grow, little by little, day by day.

Saint Faustina, pray for us!

Trust. Surrender. Believe. Receive.

LESSON

One of the great quests of the spiritual life is to align what we want with God's vision for our life. Discovering what God wants for your life rarely happens all at once. It's an unfolding process that takes time, ongoing effort, and above all, trust. Begin today. Find a quiet place where you can be alone with God, allow the silence to settle your heart and mind, and then ask: God, what do You want?

VIRTUE OF THE DAY

Devotion: The virtue of devotion consists of loyal, loving, consistent, and enthusiastic desire to please God in all things. It is a specifically religious act, chosen deliberately and freely, and directed toward God. Who or what would an outside observer deduce you are devoted to? Too many people misplace their devotion. Be careful not to misplace yours. To give something that belongs to God to anyone or anything else is a grave disorder.

DIVINE MERCY PRAYER

Eternal God, in whom mercy is endless and the treasury of compassion inexhaustible, look kindly upon us and increase Your mercy in us, that in difficult moments we might not despair nor become despondent, but with great confidence submit ourselves to Your holy will, which is Love and Mercy itself.

We Are Pilgrims of Mercy and We Are People of the Eucharist. Visit **www.ConsecrateAmerica.com** (or scan the QR code) to sign the historic petition to Consecrate America to the Eucharist!

DAY 9
JOHN PAUL II: THE HAPPIEST DAY OF MY LIFE

"Approach the throne of grace with boldness, so that we may receive mercy and find grace to help in time of need." Hebrews 4:16

What was the happiest day of Pope John Paul II's life?

We could sift through his incredible life, come up with a list of possibilities, debate their merits, and guess, but we don't have to, because on April 30, 2000, Pope John Paul II stood in St. Peter's Square before pilgrims from around the world, and spoke these words, "This is the happiest day of my life."

That was the day he canonized Sister Faustina. It was the first canonization of the New Millennium. John Paul II hoped it would usher in a new era of mercy and hope.

It was also the moment he established Divine Mercy Sunday as a universal feast for the Church. It has become just one of the many lasting legacies of his extraordinary life and papacy.

John Paul II had a special devotion to Divine Mercy throughout his life, and a special affection for Sister Faustina, who shared his Polish heritage. All this was born from his innate conviction that "There is nothing that humanity needs more than Divine Mercy."

Are these just words? Well, let's consider them from two perspectives. First, from the perspective of human need. What are our needs? Food, water, shelter, clothing, sleep, health, safety, relationships, emotional support, community, intellectual stimulation, meaning, purpose, spiritual nourishment, and so much more. But one of the greatest saints in the history of the world is saying, more than all of that, more than the air we breathe, we need mercy. We could spend the rest of our lives meditating on that single idea.

Now, let's consider the second perspective. Did Pope John Paul II align his life with his words, "There is nothing that humanity needs more than Divine Mercy"?

Mehmet Ali Ağca was born in eastern Turkey. He became a petty criminal, gang member, and a smuggler as a teenager. His crimes grew more serious with each passing year and on February 1, 1979, the twenty-one-year-old murdered the editor of a major Turkish newspaper. Ağca was captured and sentenced to life in prison but escaped six months into his sentence.

In the spring of 1981, Ann Odre, a sixty-year-old hairdresser from Buffalo, used her life savings to travel to Italy on pilgrimage. On May 13 she was in St. Peter's Square when Ağca attempted to assassinate Pope John Paul II. The terrorist fired four shots at the Pope. One bullet struck him in the hand, a second in the abdomen, and a third in the arm. He was rushed to the Gemelli Hospital in Rome.

The fourth bullet hit Ann Odre in the chest. She was in critical condition when she arrived at Santo Spirito Hospital.

The Pope and Ann both miraculously survived. Four days later, lying in his hospital bed, John Paul II gave a radio address to the world and began with these words, "I pray for the brother who struck me, whom I have sincerely forgiven. United to Christ, Priest and Victim, I offer my sufferings for the Church and for the world."

Two years later, John Paul II visited his assailant in prison and embraced him in person. His forgiveness and mercy shocked and inspired the world. It brought Divine Mercy alive for all the world to see.

The phrase "just words" doesn't apply to any aspect of Pope John Paul II's life. He was a man of towering integrity, unshakable honor, unwavering virtue, a beacon of moral excellence, and his enthusiasm to spread the faith was contagious. It was his dream that the whole world would come to know God's endless mercy. Today, you are the fulfillment of his dream.

Why was the day he instituted Divine Mercy Sunday the happiest day of Pope John Paul II's life? Because he was intimately and painfully aware of the world's need for mercy and he had a burning desire to share God's mercy with the world.

Take a few minutes in the classroom of silence today and imagine what words of encouragement Saint John Paul II would speak to you as you prepare to consecrate yourself to Divine Mercy.

Saint John Paul II, pray for us!

Trust. Surrender. Believe. Receive.

LESSON

God's mercy is the source of unimaginable happiness. We are each called to be Pilgrims of Mercy and share God's mercy with all those who cross our paths.

VIRTUE OF THE DAY

Enthusiasm: The virtue of enthusiasm leads us not just to love God and neighbor, but to vigorously seek out opportunities to do so. It reflects the state of a person's heart. Spiritual laziness leads to all manner of problems in this life and the next. Each day, choose a task that you have been avoiding or neglecting and attack it with new energy.

DIVINE MERCY PRAYER

Eternal God, in whom mercy is endless and the treasury of compassion inexhaustible, look kindly upon us and increase Your mercy in us, that in difficult moments we might not despair nor become despondent, but with great confidence submit ourselves to Your holy will, which is Love and Mercy itself.

DAY 10
AUGUSTINE: MORE BEAUTIFUL THAN EVER

"Approach the throne of grace with boldness, so that we may receive mercy and find grace to help in time of need." Hebrews 4:16

Can something that has been broken be put back together in a way that makes it more beautiful than ever before?

It may seem like an impossible proposition to our straight-line, everything-in-its-place, secular minds. But I marvel at how God doesn't use straight lines or right-angles in nature. The perfection of nature is marked by crooked lines, brokenness, seemingly imperfect colors, and things that seem out of place.

If we put on the mind of God, we discover one of the most beautiful truths this life has to offer: Something that has been devastatingly broken can be put back together in a way that makes it more beautiful than ever before. It is true for things, but it is even more true for people, and it is true for you. This truth carries with it tremendous hope.

We believe that once something is broken it can never be as beautiful as it was before. But that's not true. It's true that it cannot be exactly the same as it was before, but that doesn't mean it cannot surpass its former self. You don't look at a wonderful tree that loses some leaves and limbs in a storm, and say, "It's ruined forever." But we say that about ourselves and others.

The Japanese have a beautiful artform called Kintsugi. In our disposable culture, if we break a vase or a bowl, we throw it away and buy a new one. This simple act allows us to maintain the illusion that life is not messy. It plays into our delusion of perfection.

But life is messy, perfect is a myth, and the wisdom of the Japanese art of Kintsugi has much to teach us. It is a form of ceramics that I have been fascinated with for years. When a vase or bowl or cup is broken, artists gather up the broken pieces and glue them back together, but it is how they put them back together that is steeped in wisdom and beauty.

Japanese Kintsugi artists mix gold dust with the glue. They don't try to hide the cracks. They own them, honor them, accentuate them by making them golden. They don't pretend the vase was never broken. They celebrate the cracks as part of its story.

Can something that has been broken be put back together in a way that makes it more beautiful than ever before? Absolutely. But the more beautiful question is this: Can *someone* who has been broken be healed and become more beautiful and more lovable than ever before?

Yes. This is the redemption we celebrate in Jesus Christ and the history of Christianity is a long line of stories, one more stunning than the next, about God transforming the most unlikely people and then working through them in the most unimaginable ways.

Atop this list in the Canon of Saints is Saint Augustine. He is a staggering example of Divine Mercy at work in the human heart. "Every saint has a past, and every sinner has a future," was Oscar Wilde's observation and Augustine is certainly proof. Wherever you are in your journey, wherever you have been and whatever you have done, the lives of saints such as Augustine remind us that God never gives up on us—even if at times we give up on ourselves or give up on Him.

Augustine had given himself over to just about every pleasure and ambition that this world has to offer. But they all left him dissatisfied. His own words sum up his journey and his destination in a single line: "Our hearts are restless Lord, until they rest in you."

Imagine the moment when Augustine finally surrendered. Weary of the world's broken promises, empty in his heart and in his soul, he finally turned to God. He became aware of his great need for mercy, and just becoming aware of our need for mercy is itself a significant manifestation of mercy.

Mercy manifests in so many different ways in our lives. The clarity God gave Augustine was a powerful form of mercy, and he spent the rest of his life sharing that mercy with others. Clarity is merciful. Augustine's writings provided a bridge between Greek philosophy and Christian theology, demonstrating that faith and reason were not only compatible, but complementary. The clarity of his philosophical writings has been influencing Western thought for over fifteen hundred years.

Clear teaching is a kindness. Clear teaching is merciful. This was one of the many ways Augustine allowed God's mercy to flow through him to others.

God is the Master Potter who picks up our broken pieces and mercifully glues us back together with His gold-dust-infused glue.

Can *someone* who has been broken be healed and become more beautiful and more lovable than ever before? So many of the saints are striking reminders that the answer to this question is yes.

Wherever you are in your spiritual journey, every saint in the history of our faith wants to whisper in your ear: Today is a new day and every moment is a chance to turn it all around.

Each day we are a step closer to our consecration to Divine Mercy. Today I leave you with these words which Jesus spoke to Faustina: "I desire to pour out My divine life into human souls and sanctify them, if only they are willing to accept My grace. The greatest sinners would achieve great sanctity, if only they would trust in My mercy."

Saint Augustine, pray for us!

Trust. Surrender. Believe. Receive.

LESSON
No one is irredeemable. Today is a new day, and every moment is a chance to turn it all around. For more than two thousand years, Jesus has been radically transforming the lives of men, women, and children in every corner of the world. But that is history. Now He wants to radically transform you and your life. Are you ready?

VIRTUE OF THE DAY
Surrender: The virtue of surrender leads to tranquility. If you find yourself wrestling with every situation or doing battle with every person, it's time to explore why you are so insistent on imposing your will on every person and situation. The secret to surrendering to God is knowing your responsibilities and being clear about His responsibilities. Our willingness to surrender says a lot about our understanding of God.

DIVINE MERCY PRAYER
Eternal God, in whom mercy is endless and the treasury of compassion inexhaustible, look kindly upon us and increase Your mercy in us, that in difficult moments we might not despair nor become despondent, but with great confidence submit ourselves to Your holy will, which is Love and Mercy itself.

DAY 11
MONICA: EVERY FAMILY NEEDS A PRAYERFUL GIANT

"Approach the throne of grace with boldness, so that we may receive mercy and find grace to help in time of need." Hebrews 4:16

One of the most insidious temptations in the Christian life is the belief that prayer has no effect.

For twenty-five years, as I traveled from one country to the next, from one city to the next, one of the most acute forms of spiritual anguish I witnessed almost every day was that of mothers and fathers whose children have stopped practicing their Catholic faith. I have encountered so many parents and grandparents who are heartbroken because their children or grandchildren have left the Church.

This was the pain Saint Monica experienced. She prayed and fasted for her son Augustine's conversion. It would have been easy for Monica to lose hope and fall into despair. But she didn't because she was clear about one fundamental truth that resounds throughout the history of salvation: No person is beyond the reach of God's merciful and redeeming love.

While Augustine was selfishly pursuing his hedonistic lifestyle, following the heretical teachings of Manichaeism, and generally living a morally wayward life, his mother Monica was praying for him night and day. She is a steadfast example of unwavering faith, extraordinary patience and perseverance, trust in God's providence and timing, motherly love, and parental sacrifice.

Monica prayed like so many parents do, but she also prayed for very specific intentions. She prayed for her son's conversion to Christianity, for his release from false beliefs and heretical teachings, that his heart would be open to the beauty of the Catholic faith, for his moral transformation, that he would abandon his sinful habits and adopt a life of virtue, that God would send wise and faithful Catholics into Augustine's life, that God would be merciful to her son, and that God would give her son divine guidance.

Augustine was massively resistant to his mother's overtures and to God's promptings, but Monica never gave up hope. She didn't expect immediate results, but rather trusted in God's timing, and persevered in her prayers for her three children and her husband.

There are people who think prayer is a waste of time. Saint Monica would respectfully disagree. She was a prayerful giant. What is a prayerful giant? A prayerful giant is a person who covers their family with prayer, anchoring the family in God's grace.

We all have family members who have stopped practicing the faith. Some drift away, unaware of what they are leaving behind. Others grow jaded and reject the faith they were brought up in. Some were abused and have an understandable aversion to the Church due to the faith-wound they carry. No matter what the situation is for your family members, it can be painful and difficult to navigate. It can feel hopeless at times, but Monica is an inspiring example to keep praying.

Praying for others is merciful. Praying for those we love is a mercy that has a multi-generational impact on a family.

Every family needs a prayerful giant. Tolstoy begins the epic novel *Anna Karenina* with these lines: "Happy families are all alike; every unhappy family is unhappy in its own way." Families with great faith have a prayerful giant somewhere in their not-too-distant past. Monica was a prayerful giant. All the fruits of Augustine's writings and ministry are fruits of her prayers. Her prayers have helped millions of people in every generation for fifteen hundred years return to God.

Every time I visited one of my friends as a child, his grandmother was sitting quietly in the corner fingering her rosary beads. I didn't know it at the time, but she was a prayerful giant, immersing her family in God's love and mercy.

These prayerful giants pray constantly for their families. How far do you have to go back in your family tree to find a prayerful giant? A prayerful giant is a person who covers their family with prayer, anchoring the family in God's grace. If we want our families to have enduring, multi-generational faith, perhaps we are being called to become those prayerful giants.

We may be tempted to believe there is no hope at times, but that is never true. Don't let what you can't do interfere with what you can do, and what you can do is pray.

Even though her son rejected the faith again and again, Monica never gave up. She cried out to God, begging Him to have mercy on Augustine's soul, imploring Him to lead her son back to a life of virtue. She prayed ceaselessly for seventeen years. She became a prayerful giant. She covered her family with prayer. Little did she know the influence her prayers would eventually have on the Catholic Church around the world and every society in the Western world.

Augustine's conversion happened just one year before Monica's death. Her prayers were answered, and the generosity of God was on full display. Her request was modest compared to the overwhelming abundance of God's answer. Augustine went on to become one of the greatest saints in the history of Christianity.

And at every step along the way, Monica was growing in virtue and developing a deeper intimacy with God, which in turn led her to become a great saint.

This mother and son duo highlights the powerful influence a mother's faith can have on her children. This story demonstrates the power of prayer. How could your family tree be transformed if you become a prayerful giant?

It is a great mercy to pray for others—both the living and the dead. God invites all of us to cover our family with His grace and mercy through prayer—especially those who are yet to comprehend the genius of Catholicism.

Pray for your children, your spouse, your parents and grandparents, your grandchildren and great grandchildren. Pray for generations past and generations yet to come, deep into the future. Bestow upon your family the gift of prayer just as Monica did.

It isn't easy to pray for weeks, and months, and years. It's easy to get discouraged. It requires trust and hope to wait patiently for God's plan to unfold. But if you are persistent in prayer, you'll be amazed what God will do through your prayers. And like Monica, you'll be amazed at who you become.

Saint Monica, pray for us!

Trust. Surrender. Believe. Receive.

LESSON

Your family needs a prayerful giant. A prayerful giant is a person who covers their family with prayer, anchoring the family in God's grace. Decide right now to accept God's invitation and challenge to become your family's prayerful giant. Start praying for everyone in your extended family. But don't stop there. Research your family tree, and start praying for generations past, as far back as you can trace. And start praying for future generations—pray for the next ten generations and beyond.

VIRTUE OF THE DAY

Perseverance: Perseverance teaches us to resolve difficulties. Acquiring this virtue requires both grace and significant personal effort. There is no virtue in beginning. It is easy. Many start, few finish. This is true in almost everything. Don't look at how far you still have to go, look at how far you have come, and consider how your life would be if you had never found this path at all.

DIVINE MERCY PRAYER

Eternal God, in whom mercy is endless and the treasury of compassion inexhaustible, look kindly upon us and increase Your mercy in us, that in difficult moments we might not despair nor become despondent, but with great confidence submit ourselves to Your holy will, which is Love and Mercy itself.

DAY 12
KATHARINE DREXEL: BE BOLD. BE CATHOLIC.

"Approach the throne of grace with boldness, so that we may receive mercy and find grace to help in time of need." Hebrews 4:16

The Catholic Church is full of amazing women. Every age boasts remarkable examples of the goodness that God has placed in the hearts of women.

We read in the Scriptures, "Taste and see the goodness of the Lord" (Psalm 34:8), and "Give thanks to the Lord for He is good, His love endures forever" (1 Chronicles 34:16), and at Sunday School each week leaders call out, "God is good," and children reply, "All the time." We are well aware of the goodness of God, and we were made in the image of God. Our capacity for goodness is significant, and the power of simple goodness can change the course of history when we live our faith boldly in the service of others.

The day God placed the vision for Dynamic Catholic in my heart, I had so many questions, and what God was asking seemed impossible for so many reasons. But in my mind's eye I can still see four words I scribbled on the page that day: Be Bold. Be Catholic. We have used those words every single day to invite you, challenge you, and encourage you to step up, get involved in this great mission, and do your part in God's plan.

Be Bold. Be Catholic. It's an audacious rallying cry that has been inspiring and uniting people to do something beautiful for the Church and for today's Catholics.

Katharine Drexel embodied this call to action with wholehearted enthusiasm.

What do you know about Katharine Drexel? Born to a wealthy banking family in Philadelphia, Katharine was raised in the belief that all Christians have a responsibility to work toward the greater good. Her parents believed their wealth gave them a particular responsibility to the poor. Francis Drexel, Katharine's father, was one of the richest men in the United States, and yet, he lived modestly and dedicated a significant portion of his fortune to charitable causes.

Even though he did not become Catholic until later in his life, the charities he supported throughout his life were Catholic charities for both spiritual and practical reasons. He had enormous respect for the Catholic Church's commitment to helping the poor, providing education across a broad spectrum of society, for addressing the social issues of the day, and for imbuing ordinary people's lives with virtue. He also viewed Catholic charities as efficient, organized, and impactful, which made them a logical choice for his financial support.

His wife Hannah was deeply committed to her Catholic faith and her joy, clarity, and example had an enormous influence on her husband and her children.

Hannah died when Katharine was young, and her father remarried. Her stepmother Emma would also have a lasting impact on her life. Emma also had a robust faith life and her nurturing guidance helped shape Katharine into the strong, compassionate, devout woman who would go on to become a saint.

The unspoken expectation was that Katharine would enter society and find a suitable match for marriage. But she felt a different call on her life and began to discern a vocation to religious life.

In 1884, when Katharine was in her mid-twenties, the family made a trip out to the American West. She was shocked to witness firsthand the plight of the Native Americans. Poverty was rampant. Living conditions were atrocious. Tuberculosis, smallpox, and measles were ravaging the Native population. Classrooms were overcrowded and teachers were few. The seed of a powerful mission was planted in Katharine's heart.

The family returned home, but less than a year later Katharine's father passed away suddenly. Devastated by yet another loss, Katharine and her sisters embarked on a tour of Europe. It was during this trip that Katharine had a private audience with Pope Leo XIII. Wrestling with the call to a contemplative religious life and her desire to serve the neglected and forgotten, Katharine asked the Pope to consider founding a congregation that could serve the indigenous population in America.

The Pope's response to Katharine rocked her to her core: "Why not be a missionary yourself, my child?"

By the time Katharine reached the room outside the Pope's chambers she knew what she had to do. Katharine left home, joined the Sisters of Mercy in Pittsburgh, and then used her inheritance to found the Sisters of the Blessed Sacrament, a religious order dedicated to serving minority groups.

Over the next sixty years, Mother Drexel established more than sixty schools and missions, primarily for African Americans and Native Americans, living in a society riddled with racism and segregation. She founded Xavier University in New Orleans, the first Catholic university in the United States for African Americans. It is also the first Catholic university founded by a saint, and today serves 3,500 students each year. The Sisters of the Blessed Sacrament had grown to five hundred members in fifty-one convents by the time of Mother Drexel's death, and their mission to serve underprivileged minorities continues to this day.

She believed in the power of simple goodness. Goodness was at the heart of Katharine Drexel's life, spirituality, and mission. The goodness of God and our ability to share His goodness by joyfully serving other people.

Her spirit lives on in her words:

"We must attract people by joy in order to lead them to goodness."

"Kindness is the natural fruit of goodness of the heart."

"If we wish to serve God and love our neighbor well, we must manifest our joy in the service we render to Him and them. Let us open wide our hearts. It is joy which invites us. Press forward and fear nothing."

"Ours is the spirit of the Eucharist, the total gift of self."

"Peacefully do at each moment what at that moment ought to be done."

"Lord, teach me to love others as you love me."

These quotes highlight Katharine Drexel's focus on living a life of joyful service, self-giving, and spreading goodness wherever we go.

Be Bold. Be Catholic. Katharine Drexel was bold in so many ways. She rejected the comfortable life society intended for her. She gave up her inheritance. She boldly followed God's call even when it meant ignoring social norms. She was passionately serving the marginalized and minorities as a white woman seventy years before the Civil Rights Movement.

How boldly are you living your faith? How completely Catholic are you? Katharine Drexel was a bold visionary with a heart that was Catholic through and through.

It's time to live our faith more boldly.

Saint Katharine Drexel, pray for us!

Trust. Surrender. Believe. Receive.

LESSON

Mission is where our talents and passions collide with the needs of others and the world. The worldly scope and scale of your unique mission is irrelevant. All that matters is that you embrace and carry out the mission God has called you to.

VIRTUE OF THE DAY

Generosity: The virtue of generosity mirrors the abundance of God's generosity. Give something away every day. It need not be a material possession or money. Give a compliment, a smile, advice, encouragement. Express your appreciation. Catch someone doing something right. Give everywhere you go to everyone you meet. Live a life of staggering generosity.

DIVINE MERCY PRAYER

Eternal God, in whom mercy is endless and the treasury of compassion inexhaustible, look kindly upon us and increase Your mercy in us, that in difficult moments we might not despair nor become despondent, but with great confidence submit ourselves to Your holy will, which is Love and Mercy itself.

DAY 13
DAMIEN OF MOLOKAI: RADICAL COMPASSION

"Approach the throne of grace with boldness, so that we may receive mercy and find grace to help in time of need." Hebrews 4:16

Imagine for a moment the life of the average twenty-four-year-old.

At the age of twenty-four, Damien of Molokai volunteered to leave his homeland of Belgium to serve as a missionary in the Kingdom of Hawaii where he was ordained a priest. Eleven years later he volunteered to go to the island of Molokai, where those with leprosy were forcibly quarantined. He knew the risks and he went anyway.

Damien worked tirelessly to improve living conditions for the patients. He helped them build homes, schools, a church, and a hospital. He provided medical care, organized the community, and restored dignity to the patients. He ministered to both their physical needs and spiritual well-being, offering the sacraments, and sharing in their suffering.

After serving the rejected and suffering people of Molokai for many years, Damien contracted leprosy himself. The year was 1884 and he was forty-four years old. Despite his declining health, he continued his work until he died five years later.

Pope Benedict XVI canonized Damien on October 11, 2009, recognizing him as a "Martyr of Charity" and a model of self-sacrificial love.

The radical compassion of Saint Damien of Molokai was so Christlike that I have trouble comprehending it. And most of the letters he wrote were burned upon arrival, out of fear that leprosy could be transmitted just by touching them. So, I tried to imagine what he would say to you as you make this consecration journey, and this is what I came up with:

My dear brothers and sisters in Christ,

The love of Christ compels us to go where others fear to tread, to embrace those whom the world has cast aside, and to pour ourselves out in service to the most vulnerable. This is the essence of radical compassion—a love that knows no boundaries, a mercy that seeks no reward, and a commitment that endures even in the face of great personal suffering.

During my years on the island of Molokai, living among those afflicted by leprosy, I learned firsthand what it means to live out this radical compassion. It is a call to see Christ in the face of the suffering, to love with a heart that does not count the cost, and to give until nothing is left but the joy of having served.

When I first arrived at the leper colony, I was struck by the immense suffering of the people. These men, women, and children had been torn from their families and left to fend for themselves in isolation. Their bodies bore the disfigurements of disease, but it was their loneliness, rejection, and despair that cut the deepest wounds.

Yet, as I walked among them, I was reminded of Christ's words: "Whatever you did for one of the least of these brothers and sisters of mine, you did for me." (Matthew 25:40) In their pain, I saw the suffering Christ. In their isolation, I saw the Christ who was abandoned on the Cross. And in their cries for help, I heard the voice of Christ calling me to love without hesitation.

To practice radical compassion is to recognize the dignity of every human being, especially those whom society has marginalized. It is to see beyond appearances, beyond fear, and beyond prejudice, and to embrace each person as a beloved child of God.

Radical compassion requires a willingness to go beyond the limits of comfort and convenience. It is not a love that remains distant or detached; it is a love that gets its hands dirty, that suffers alongside others, and that offers everything it has.

When I chose to live among the lepers of Molokai, I did so because I believed that love demands presence. I could not merely preach to them from afar; I needed to share in their lives, their struggles, and their hopes. I built churches, heard confessions, bandaged wounds, and buried the dead. Over time, I became one of them—not just in spirit but also in body, as I eventually contracted leprosy myself.

Some may see this as a tragedy, but I see it as a gift. To suffer with those I served was to share in the very heart of Christ's mission. Jesus Himself took on our humanity, entered into our pain, and gave His life for our salvation. Radical compassion calls us to imitate this self-giving love, to be willing to lose ourselves so that others might find life.

To love radically is to live fully. It is to find meaning and purpose in the service of others and to experience the joy of being an instrument of God's mercy.

The world today is in desperate need of radical compassion. There is so much division, prejudice, and indifference toward the suffering of others. The example of Jesus and the call of the Gospel challenge us to break down these barriers and to love boldly and unconditionally.

Radical compassion does not require extraordinary circumstances. It begins in the small acts of kindness we show to our neighbors, the sacrifices we make for our families, and the openness we extend to strangers. It is a way of life that sees every person as worthy of love and every moment as an opportunity to serve.

It's not an easy path, but it is the way of Christ, and in living out this call, we not only transform the lives of others, we also draw closer to the heart of God ourselves.

Open your heart to the radical compassion of Christ. Go to Jesus in the Blessed Sacrament and He will give you the strength for whatever He calls you to. Let His love flow through you to heal this broken world. It is only by loving without limits that we find the true meaning of our lives.

Father Damien

That is what I imagine he would say to us.

Saint Damien of Molokai, pray for us!

Trust. Surrender. Believe. Receive.

LESSON

Be willing to go wherever God calls you and do whatever He asks you to do, including doing what you are doing right now, right where you are.

VIRTUE OF THE DAY

Compassion: *Compassion* comes from the Latin word *compati*, meaning to "suffer with." The virtue of compassion isn't merely acknowledging someone's suffering. It's sharing in that person's suffering.

DIVINE MERCY PRAYER

Eternal God, in whom mercy is endless and the treasury of compassion inexhaustible, look kindly upon us and increase Your mercy in us, that in difficult moments we might not despair nor become despondent, but with great confidence submit ourselves to Your holy will, which is Love and Mercy itself.

DAY 14
VINCENT DE PAUL:
GOODNESS NEVER DIES

"Approach the throne of grace with boldness, so that we may receive mercy and find grace to help in time of need." Hebrews 4:16

The saints are always around us, and their lives are intertwined with each other's and with ours.

During my last couple of years of high school, the students would take turns visiting a homeless shelter in the seediest part of Sydney. The men were homeless primarily because of alcoholism. The place was called Matt Talbot's and was run by the Society of Saint Vincent de Paul. We would visit on Friday nights, serve the men their dinner, and then sit and talk to them. My introverted self didn't like it at all.

But this is how Vincent de Paul, Frédéric Ozanam, Rosalie Rendu, and Matt Talbot entered my life, and they have never been too far from me, each for their own reasons.

Vincent de Paul was a Catholic priest in France who was ordained in 1600 and dedicated his life to serving the poor. Known for his humility, compassion, and generosity, he was widely loved and admired by the people of his time.

Frédéric Ozanam was a French scholar, journalist, and equal rights advocate. While at university, he gathered with his fellow students each week to debate various topics. One week the conversation turned to the Catholic Church. Some began to argue that while the Church had once been a source of good, it no longer was.

One student issued the challenge that would forever change Frédéric's life and the lives of millions of men and women around the world: "What is your Church doing now? What is she doing for the poor of Paris? Show us your works and we will believe you!" Frédéric reflected on the angry student's words and could not find fault with what he had said. At that moment he decided a major theme of his life would be serving the poorest people in Paris. But he had no idea how to begin. He knew where to find the city's poor, but he didn't know how to approach them, what they needed most, or how best to help them.

His reading led him to be inspired by a priest who had lived in France two hundred years earlier, Vincent de Paul. Further reading led him to discover that one of Vincent's followers, Sister Rosalie Rendu, was currently serving the poor in the slums of Paris. Frédéric approached Sister Rendu and asked her to help him and his fellow students develop a method to serve the poor that could easily be taught to more and more students over time. "Where are these fellow students?" she asked.

"They will come," he replied, though he wasn't sure they would.

The other students did come. Inspired by Frédéric's appeal to them, Sister Rendu mentored them and helped them develop a method to serve the poor. This would become the method that the Society of Saint Vincent de Paul uses even to this day in dozens of countries around the world. It focuses on visiting the poor in their homes, assessing their needs, and discerning how the society can best help each person or family.

Frédéric Ozanam ultimately founded the Society of Saint Vincent de Paul. He did it out of humility and a deep sense of gratitude to both the man who inspired him to believe it was possible to effectively serve the poor, and the woman who mentored him and his friends in the practical realities of that work: Vincent de Paul and Sister Rosalie Rendu.

Matt Talbot was an Irish dock worker, and an alcoholic from the age of twelve. When he was twenty-eight, he pledged never to drink alcohol again, and he kept that pledge for the next forty years, until his death. He spent those forty years working hard, paying back his debts, giving everything he had to the poor, sleeping on nothing but a wooden plank, and praying for several hours a day.

After his death, Talbot became an icon of Ireland's temperance movement, and his story spread around the world. He is quoted as saying, "Never be too hard on the man who can't give up drink. It's as hard to give up the drink as it is to raise the dead to life again. But both are possible and even easy for Our Lord. We have only to depend on him." Today one of Dublin's bridges bears his name, as do many addiction clinics and homeless shelters around the world, from Warsaw to Nebraska to Sydney.

And that is how at seventeen years of age I found myself feeding the poor and talking to a group of homeless men on a Friday night. I didn't know it at the time, but I was being taught one of the most difficult yet essential lessons of the Christian life: We are called to have a relationship with the poor.

Do you have a relationship with the poor? If we want to have a personal relationship with God, a personal relationship with the poor is vital.

The good we do is never lost; it never dies. The good we do lives on in other people, in other places, and in other times. We saw that with John Newton and his role in the abolition of slavery and we see a similar ripple effect from the life of Vincent de Paul. Nearly five hundred years ago he set out to serve the poor in his own place and time. His goodness has been echoing in the lives of other men and women ever since, including my own.

No act of mercy can ever be considered small. No act of love is insignificant. Each act of love and mercy has historic implications. Everything God created in the universe and beyond is connected. Our Holy Moments let out a holy ripple effect around the world. And our Holy Moments reverberate around the world in ways we cannot imagine.

There are plenty of reasons to feel discouraged, overwhelmed, powerless, and frustrated in today's world, but no amount of darkness can overcome the light. Vincent de Paul, Frédéric Ozanam, Sister Rosalie Rendu, and Matt Talbot all faced tremendous discouragement at times. It would have been so easy to give up, to retreat into a comfortable life. But they didn't. They pressed on, persevering in humble service, and the good they did lives on today.

Saint Vincent de Paul, pray for us!

Trust. Surrender. Believe. Receive.

LESSON

Everything God created in the universe and beyond is connected in ways beyond our comprehension. Our unholy moments have unholy ripple effects on the world, and our Holy Moments reverberate around the world in ways we cannot imagine. The good we do is never lost. It never dies. The good we do lives on in other people, in other places, and in other times.

VIRTUE OF THE DAY

Courage: The virtue of courage is moral strength in the face of danger or difficulty, especially in the face of anything that opposes our faith. Courage allows us to stand in our fears and do what is good, right, just, and noble. Everything significant in life requires courage.

DIVINE MERCY PRAYER

Eternal God, in whom mercy is endless and the treasury of compassion inexhaustible, look kindly upon us and increase Your mercy in us, that in difficult moments we might not despair nor become despondent, but with great confidence submit ourselves to Your holy will, which is Love and Mercy itself.

DAY 15
FEED THE HUNGRY

"Blessed are the merciful, for they will receive mercy." Matthew 5:7

The year was 1979.

A sixty-nine-year-old woman, just four foot eleven inches tall, stepped forward to receive the Nobel Peace Prize. Despite her modest height, she was a towering figure, her face instantly recognizable as one of the most famous women in the world. It was Mother Teresa.

The audience was made up of Norwegian royalty, the Nobel Committee, international leaders, dignitaries and diplomats, religious and humanitarian leaders, and the whole world via television. Her mere presence had the power to silence a room, but on this occasion, she was met with a thunderous standing ovation.

What would Mother Teresa say? There was massive speculation. It would be one of the most listened to speeches in history.

"Let us all together thank God for this beautiful occasion where we can all together proclaim the joy of spreading peace," she began. The crowd fell silent and listened with awe. Mother Teresa shared how the mercy of God was central to her ministry with this story:

One evening, a man came to the Mother House in Calcutta, and explained to Mother Teresa and the other sisters, "There is a Hindu family and the eight children have not eaten for a long time. Do something for them."

"I took rice, and I went immediately," Mother Teresa explained, "and there was this mother and her children, with shining eyes from sheer hunger. The mother took the rice from my hands and divided it into two portions. She gave one portion to her children and then she left the house."

When the mother came back, Mother Teresa asked her, "Where did you go? What did you do?"

"The Muslim family next door, they are also hungry," the mother explained.

"What surprised me most was not that she gave the rice," Mother Teresa noted in her speech, "but that in her suffering, in her hunger, she knew that somebody else was hungry, and she had the courage to share."

Mother Teresa's witness that night was mesmerizing. Not because she was putting on a show for one night, but because it was a reflection of her life. Her life was mesmerizing, and yet so much of the world looked away. I hope you and I won't look away as we explore the seven Corporal Works of Mercy this week.

One billion people on our planet are chronically hungry. This is the sanitized term we use to avoid saying they are starving to death. Twenty-five thousand people die every day of hunger, in this world, in our day and age, on our watch. By the time you finish reading this sentence, someone, somewhere in the world, will have died of starvation. And you don't have to go to the other side of the world to find people who are starving. In the United States, 47 million people face food insecurity, including one in five children. How is that possible? And still, we are constantly congratulating ourselves on the progress we have made.

There are a lot of people hungry just for food. I know the problem is more complicated than just giving them food. I just pray we have the courage to stare the problem in the face, the compassion not to look away.

Skip a meal today and meditate on what it is like to be desperately and hopelessly hungry. Meditate on these words:

"'Come, O blessed of my Father, inherit the kingdom prepared for you from the foundation of the world; for I was hungry and you gave me food, I was thirsty and you gave me drink, I was a stranger and you welcomed me, I was naked and you clothed me, I was sick and you visited me, I was in prison and you came to me.'" (Matthew 25:34-36)

Mercy is love reaching out to misery. There is so much misery in this world. We need to do more.

Our awareness of other people's hunger can be dulled by our own hunger. We may not be hungry for food, but hunger for food is only one of the many forms of hunger that plague our world. Mother Teresa observed, "We think sometimes that poverty is only being hungry, naked, and homeless. The poverty of being unwanted, unloved, and uncared for is the greatest poverty." She also wrote, "There is a terrible hunger for love. We all experience that in our lives—the pain and the loneliness. We must have the courage to recognize it. The poor you may have right in your own family. Find them. Love them."

There are so many types of hunger: physical hunger; emotional hunger; spiritual hunger; hunger for knowledge; hunger for truth; the existential hunger for meaning and purpose; hunger for peace; hunger for justice; and as Mother Teresa points out, we are all hungry for love.

Do you know what you are hungry for? We are all hungry for something. Figuring out what we are really hungry for is one of the great spiritual quests of life. To be human is to be hungry.

It takes an incredible spiritual awareness to work out what we are really hungry for. We may think that our hunger is for one thing, but once we have had our fill of that thing, we discover that the hunger is still there and deeper than ever.

Growing spiritual awareness leads us to the understanding that every yearning is in some mysterious way a yearning for God. God speaks to us in our hunger. He uses our hunger to teach us and guide us—and He speaks to us through other people's hunger.

Mercy is always an invitation to a better life, in large ways and small ways.

Feeding the hungry isn't just about food—it's about nourishing hope, restoring dignity, and sharing the love that transforms lives. Mercy is love reaching out to misery. Feeding the hungry is mercy in action.

Saint Teresa of Calcutta, pray for us!

Trust. Surrender. Believe. Receive.

LESSON

It's a horrible thing to be physically hungry. It is a hundred times worse if you cannot feed your children. We have a significant responsibility as Christians to feed the hungry. It is also important to our spiritual journey to get in touch with our own hunger.

VIRTUE OF THE DAY

Sacrifice: The virtue of sacrifice enhances the meaning of our existence. The ability to set aside our desires and personal preferences, expecting nothing in return, is evidence of the nobility of the human person. Let your selfishness give way to love and you will embrace the sacrifices of daily life enthusiastically.

DIVINE MERCY PRAYER

Eternal God, in whom mercy is endless and the treasury of compassion inexhaustible, look kindly upon us and increase Your mercy in us, that in difficult moments we might not despair nor

become despondent, but with great confidence submit ourselves to Your holy will, which is Love and Mercy itself.

DAY 16
GIVE DRINK TO THE THIRSTY

"Blessed are the merciful, for they will receive mercy." Matthew 5:7

Water is essential to life.

The stages of dehydration are brutal. One day without water and you will experience dry mouth, fatigue, and a thirst that prevents you from thinking about anything else. Two days without water and you develop headaches, dizziness, confusion, rapid heartbeat, and decreased blood pressure. By day three without water you experience severe fatigue, the inability to sweat or urinate, and organ failure. Seventy percent of the world's population wouldn't survive three days without water.

Our society has become obsessed with bottled water. There are 2,735 bottled water companies in the United States alone. Bottled water was a $300 billion industry in 2022 and is expected to be a $500 billion industry by 2032.

And while our obsession with bottled water grows, there are two billion people on the planet who don't have safe drinking water in their homes. Two billion people, in this world, in our day and age, on our watch. Seven hundred million people lack access to clean water altogether. The other 1.3 billion must walk inhumane distances to access safe drinking water.

Let me tell you a story. Meliyio is a thirty-five-year-old mother of six children in Kenya. She walks fifteen miles each day to collect water. This takes six hours each day. Her family needs about 10 gallons of water a day, but 10 gallons of water weighs 90 pounds and Meliyio can only carry 5 gallons on her own. So often her family goes without the water they desperately need.

In more than one hundred countries around the world, people wake up every day and their most urgent question surrounds obtaining enough water to survive the day. Meliyio's story is tragically common. There are millions of women like her around the world.

The burden of finding and collecting water for their families falls overwhelmingly on women and their daughters of all ages, and this has a devastating impact on their opportunities for education. On average, women in developing countries walk 3.5 miles a day, carrying 5 gallons of water, weighing approximately 45 pounds. But most of the world continues to look away.

This Corporal Work of Mercy to Give Drink to the Thirsty calls us to address this fundamental human need, not just as an act of charity, but as a response to the sacred dignity of every person. Living this Work of Mercy today requires compassion, action, and a commitment to human justice.

Jesus said to the righteous, "For I was thirsty and you gave me drink." (Matthew 25:35) These words remind us that meeting the needs of the thirsty is more than an act of kindness. It is an encounter with Christ Himself. When we quench another's thirst, we are not merely providing water. We are offering hope, dignity, mercy and love.

When Jesus was on the Cross, He cried out, "I thirst." (John 19:28) In response to His desperate plea the soldiers gave Him wine mixed with gall. This bitter combination would have only increased His dehydration and added to His misery.

There is a disturbing truth to face in all this. I cannot help but think that we are treating the people who are desperate for clean water the same way the soldiers treated Jesus. They cry out in thirst and our response leaves a bitter taste. And in all this, the Gospel continues to challenge me to radically alter the way I am living my life.

Thirst is a major issue in our world. You may feel called to do something about it. If so, donate to a charity, volunteer, or go on a mission trip focused on helping people get access to clean water. But the rest of us shouldn't make the mistake of thinking we can't live out this Work of Mercy, because as we discovered with hunger, there are many forms of thirst.

We meet people every day who are crying out, "I thirst." They may not lack access to clean water, but their souls are dying of thirst. And the culture gives them wine mixed with gall, which only increases their dehydration and adds to their misery.

We are each thirsty in our own ways. You know your thirst, and I know mine. Your thirst may be different next week, and it may be the same. But the reality is our souls are thirsty—and we cannot satisfy a spiritual thirst with a worldly potion.

Most people in our culture are severely spiritually dehydrated. Our spiritual thirst is real and isn't going away. Giving drink to the thirsty also means quenching people's spiritual thirst.

The challenge of clean water was a significant issue during Jesus' time also. He wasn't indifferent to people's need for water to quench their physical thirst, but He also called attention to their spiritual thirst.

Jesus speaks about living water in the Gospel of John, saying, "Let anyone who is thirsty come to me and drink. As the Scripture has said, 'Out of the believer's heart rivers of living water will flow.'" (John 7:37-38)

Mercy is always an invitation to a better life, in large ways and small ways.

We have a responsibility to attend to our own spiritual thirst, to dig a well by developing a robust prayer life. By developing a daily practice of prayer and reflection. That's how we dig the well.

Once we have dug our own well, we can help others to do the same. Teach someone how to pray, teach someone about Holy

Moments, start a prayer group, host a Bible study, invite someone to go to Adoration with you, give someone a great spiritual book. There are so many practical ways to help other people gain access to the living water they so desperately need.

It is no coincidence that the image of Divine Mercy shows streams of crystal-clear water flowing from the heart of Jesus. Mercy is love reaching out to misery. He wants His living waters to gush forth into the world and hydrate every soul.

Trust. Surrender. Believe. Receive.

LESSON

There are two billion people on the planet who don't have safe drinking water in their homes. This stands as an indictment of our humanity and our Christianity. Beyond physical thirst, most people in our culture are severely spiritually dehydrated. Our spiritual thirst is real and isn't going away.

VIRTUE OF THE DAY

Spiritual Awareness: The virtue of spiritual awareness is marked by a sensitivity to the presence of God. It makes us mindful of how different people, things, and experiences unite us with God or draw us away from Him.

DIVINE MERCY PRAYER

Eternal God, in whom mercy is endless and the treasury of compassion inexhaustible, look kindly upon us and increase Your mercy in us, that in difficult moments we might not despair nor become despondent, but with great confidence submit ourselves to Your holy will, which is Love and Mercy itself.

Help your friends and family discover the power of Holy Moments. Request your six FREE copies of Matthew Kelly's bestseller *Holy Moments* today!
Visit **www.HolyMomentsBook.com** or scan the QR code.

DAY 17
CLOTHE THE NAKED

"Blessed are the merciful, for they will receive mercy." Matthew 5:7

What would you think if you saw a monk walk into a brothel?

Vitalis of Gaza was an Egyptian hermit in the seventh century. After many years in the desert, at the age of sixty, he left the desert for the city of Alexandria.

He worked as a day laborer, toiling tirelessly at grueling tasks to earn a wage. At the end of each day, he would go to the local brothel, where he spent his earnings. Night after night, the former hermit was seen with a different prostitute. The local Christians were understandably scandalized. Vitalis was openly mocked and humiliated. Many of Alexandria's Christians petitioned the Patriarch to excommunicate him, but the Patriarch was unwilling to act on unverified rumors.

One day Vitalis was viciously attacked and killed. Some judgmental Christians of Alexandria felt a sense of relief when news spread. But then something unexpected happened. Dozens of former prostitutes attended his funeral.

The curious Patriarch had questions. His questions led to a stunning revelation: The women professed that Vitalis had saved both their lives and their souls.

Vitalis wasn't as debauched as the people of Alexandria assumed. Each night, after paying for a woman's services, he would lovingly tell her he had bought her a night of rest for her body and soul. Every night he would give the woman his own food, and then, while she rested, Vitalis kept vigil over her, praying for her all night.

Who was this man and what were his true intentions? the women wondered. It took some hours to fall asleep out of fear. They could not comprehend his kindness and generosity. But the next morning, after their first peaceful night in years, the women asked Vitalis why he was doing this. He told them his story and talked about God's love and mercy.

Mercy is always an invitation to a better life, in large ways and small ways.

Vitalis' actions had a profound effect on many of the women and they asked him to help them escape their lives as prostitutes. The former hermit arranged marriages, provided dowries, and secured places for some in monasteries.

A vow of silence was the only request he made of these women. Vitalis knew that if word spread about what he was doing, the people who controlled the brothels would no longer give him access to the women he felt called to serve.

Vitalis willingly suffered public shame, disgrace, and humiliation. He sacrificed his reputation for the sake of these women who society abhorred. This is a radical humility. Would you sacrifice your good name to save souls? Would you be willing to suffer silently while people ridiculed you?

Clothing the naked wasn't just about physical clothes for Vitalis, it was also about clothing these women, who had been mercilessly dehumanized, with human dignity.

Dehumanization takes many forms. Some things are dehumanizing by their very nature, for example, violence, slavery, abuse, injustice, torture, poverty, discrimination, gossip, objectification and genocide. There are many other things that can be dehumanizing, such as: work, technology, debt, humor, laws, entertainment, social media, and even education. Anytime the value and individuality of a person are being denied, that person is being stripped of their worth, their reputation, and their self-esteem.

Rehumanization is an effort to reverse the effects of dehumanization by restoring human dignity, helping each and every person develop a healthy sense of self, and reprioritizing people above money, objects, systems, and institutions. Rehumanization is about learning to be human again, which may sound strange, but it's amazing how often and in how many ways the average person experiences dehumanization.

Mercy is rehumanizing. Giving and receiving mercy helps us rediscover our humanity and to see ourselves as God's precious children. Vitalis was on a merciful quest to rehumanize these women. He was desperately trying to show them how deeply God loved them.

Rehumanization. Is there any more urgent task before society today? Which of our problems would not be solved by seeing each other as human beings?

The future will be profoundly human or not at all. There will be no future unless we rediscover what it means to be human. I would argue that it is impossible to solve the problems we face as a society unless we undertake a great rehumanization, clothing each person with the protection of human dignity.

The call to clothe the naked begins with material clothes. How much clothing do you have that you never wear? We should donate clothes we no longer need, but we should also become more conscientious consumers. Before we buy more clothes, we should consider if the money could be better spent clothing the naked in some other way.

And, like Vitalis, we should look for new and innovative ways to clothe the naked. Eradicating pornography from our society would be one place to start. Our culture has been pornified. The dehumanizing effects of pornography are insidious, rampant, and having an incalculable impact on every relationship in our society.

A Pilgrim of Mercy inhabits that difficult and exhilarating space between the physical and the spiritual. Clothe the Naked. This Work of Mercy also challenges us to consider ways we may be creating nakedness. We should diligently avoid stripping people of their dignity with our words, our choices, and our actions. Eradicating gossip from our conversations is also a great place to start. Gossip is one of the easiest ways to strip other people of their dignity.

Mercy is love reaching out to misery. It's time to clothe the naked with a great rehumanization movement.

Saint Vitalis, pray for us!

Trust. Surrender. Believe. Receive.

LESSON

There are people in every country who need our help to clothe their nakedness. Around the world and here at home, the effects of dehumanization in all its forms have stripped millions of their dignity. It is time to rehumanize the human family. The future of humanity depends upon it. There are many ways to clothe the naked.

VIRTUE OF THE DAY

Kindness: The virtue of kindness is the excellence of character that imbues every thought, word, and action with goodness. It reveals the essence of our humanity in our ability to bring the goodness of God into any situation. Never underestimate the value of a kind word, thought, or deed. The power of simple kindness is unfathomable. The future of humanity is dependent on the selfless caring we call kindness.

DIVINE MERCY PRAYER

Eternal God, in whom mercy is endless and the treasury of compassion inexhaustible, look kindly upon us and increase Your mercy in us, that in difficult moments we might not despair nor become despondent, but with great confidence submit ourselves to Your holy will, which is Love and Mercy itself.

DAY 18
SHELTER THE HOMELESS

"Blessed are the merciful, for they will receive mercy." Matthew 5:7

Professor Williams taught at a small Catholic college. One of the freshman classes he taught was Christian Moral Principles. Year after year, he grew increasingly frustrated that his students were more interested in their grades than living the central principles of their faith.

More than being irritated by his students' attitudes, he felt he was failing in his duty to educate them. The mid-semester exam made up 50 percent of their final grade, so after ten years he decided to try a new approach.

When the students arrived at the classroom for the mid-term exam, they found a notice on the locked door informing them that the exam had been moved to a different classroom on the other side of campus.

The students were all of a sudden flustered. They rushed to the other side of campus. The small building where the exam was now being held had only one entrance and there was a homeless man laying across the entrance.

"He's asleep," one student said. "He stinks," said another. "Step over him," one young man suggested. But they discovered they couldn't open the door without hitting the homeless man. "Wake him," someone said. "I'm not touching him," his friend replied. "Is he dead?" someone asked. "Let's call security," another student suggested. "Maybe we should call 911," was their last idea before one of their classmates said, "Guys, this way, there's a janitor's entrance around back."

Inside the classroom there read a message on the board that explained the exam would start a little late to give everyone time to get across campus.

Ten minutes later the homeless man walked into the classroom. It was their professor disguised as a homeless man.

"The homeless man was your exam," Professor Williams explained. "Needless to say, you all failed." The students began to murmur and complain, but their professor continued, "At the heart of Jesus' life and teachings we find a profound mercy. It is difficult to comprehend, but we all need it. We don't deserve it, but God gives it to us abundantly nonetheless. And to live the Gospel means to carry this mercy into the world and share it with those who cross our paths, or in this case, block our paths." The students moaned.

"That's 50 percent of our grade," one student called out.

"Yes," the professor replied.

"We're all going to fail the class," another commented with disdain.

"You deserve to fail and that would be justice, but as I am trying to teach you the compassion of Christ, His deep and abiding mercy, I am going to offer a make-up exam."

A wave of relief swept through the classroom.

"Over the next ten days, I would like you to get to know a homeless person and write a paper listing ten surprising things you learn about that person."

When the students returned after the mid-semester break, the quality of the discussions in class improved for the rest of the year.

What would have to happen for you to end up living on the streets?

My older brother Andrew worked for a nonprofit organization in Australia that provided crisis accommodation and helped the homeless rebuild their lives and reintegrate into society.

One day at lunch he said something that stunned me: "Most people are only three events away from becoming homeless."

"Say that again," I asked for clarity.

"We refer to it as the rule of three," my brother explained. "Most people become extremely vulnerable to homelessness if they experience three of the more stressful life events in a short period of time. Job loss, the death of a loved one, divorce, chronic illness, a serious injury at work, unexpected medical expenses, domestic violence, eviction, loss of housing, or even moving."

"Why moving?" I asked.

"That's the crazy one. It's not much spoken about. A family moves and one partner locks the other out during the move to instigate separation as a step toward divorce," Andrew explained.

Forty percent of Americans are just one paycheck, unexpected medical bill, or job loss away from financial instability. When it comes to homelessness specifically, it's estimated that about 25-40 percent of people could be vulnerable to homelessness if they experience three major stressors.

My brother further explained, "We used this rule of three as a heuristic to remove judgement from our hearts and minds."

The reason it's so easy to judge homeless people is because we see them as different—dirty, smelly, irresponsible, lazy, dangerous, etc. The reason it is so easy to ignore homeless people is because we don't see them as our neighbor.

A lot of people point to addiction and mental illness as the primary causes of homelessness, but it isn't that simple. Sometimes addiction and mental illness lead to homelessness, and sometimes homelessness leads to addiction and mental illness. It is a vicious cycle. And addictions and mental illnesses that were manageable with stable housing and work often become unmanageable on the streets. Think about the emotions that come with homelessness: fear, shame, hopelessness, loneliness, frustration, depression, anxiety, and guilt. These are enough to test any person's mental health and would drive most people to some form of substance abuse.

The Department of Housing and Urban Development reports that at least 771,480 men, women, and children are homeless in the United States today. Are we really okay with that?

Who is my neighbor? Our collective answer to this single question directs human history. When Jesus was asked the question, He famously replied with the parable of the Good Samaritan. (Luke 10: 29-37) Living out the Corporal Works of Mercy and the Spiritual Works of Mercy is our answer to this question.

The world is full of desperate need and destructive want. When we put our wants ahead of other people's needs, we abandon our humanity.

Who is my neighbor? This simple question challenges our morality, our ethics, our virtue, our worldview, and it challenges who we think we are. I have spent countless hours pondering this question and this is the conclusion I have reached: When most people ask the question, they are usually looking to exclude someone, but the more we grow in wisdom and holiness, the more people we tend to include in our answer to this question. And for the saints, there were no strangers, just neighbors.

The mandate of Divine Mercy is to continually expand our definition of neighbor until no one stands outside the circle of our compassion. Shelter the Homeless. This Corporal Work of Mercy is an invitation to expand the definition of who we consider to be our neighbors.

Mercy is always an invitation to a better life, in large ways and small ways.

Homelessness is an enormous problem, but you shouldn't let what you can't do interfere with what you can do. You can volunteer at a homeless shelter. You can help out at a soup kitchen. You can buy a homeless person a meal. You can carry a granola bar and a bottle of water with you to give to a homeless person. You can humanize the interaction by asking the homeless person his or her name. There is so much you can do.

Mercy is love reaching out to misery, and love of neighbor is proof that we love God.

Trust. Surrender. Believe. Receive.

LESSON

Our answer to one question directs human history: Who is my neighbor? This question challenges our morality, our ethics, our virtue, our worldview, and our Christianity. The more we grow in wisdom and holiness, the more people we tend to include in our answer to this question. The mandate of Divine Mercy is to continually expand our definition of neighbor until no one stands outside the circle of our compassion.

VIRTUE OF THE DAY

Hospitality: The virtue of hospitality is the practice of warmly welcoming, generously providing for, and graciously caring for our guests and others in need.

DIVINE MERCY PRAYER

Eternal God, in whom mercy is endless and the treasury of compassion inexhaustible, look kindly upon us and increase Your mercy in us, that in difficult moments we might not despair nor become despondent, but with great confidence submit ourselves to Your holy will, which is Love and Mercy itself. Amen.

DAY 19
VISIT THE SICK

"Blessed are the merciful, for they will receive mercy." Matthew 5:7

The call to Visit the Sick is one of the most profound expressions of love and compassion that Christianity gave birth to. We perhaps cannot imagine it any other way, but this pillar of Western culture has not always existed as we know it today.

Where were the sick people when Jesus was alive? Were they in hospitals? No. Why? There were no hospitals. The sick were huddled along the side roads and on the outskirts of town. They had been abandoned by family and friends who were afraid they would also become sick.

Hospitals emerged in response to Jesus' teachings. The Gospel is a radical invitation to kindness, compassion, generosity, and mercy. Healthcare as we know it today is one of the many fruits of the Gospel, one of the many ways Christianity changed the world.

The call to care for the sick is deeply rooted in Scripture. In the Gospel of Matthew, Jesus identifies visiting the sick as a direct way of serving Him: "I was sick, and you visited me." (Matthew 25:36) The early Christians took Jesus' words seriously, and their legacy was passed from one generation to the next.

Two hundred years after the death and Resurrection of Jesus, a deadly plague broke out across Rome and the surrounding region. The healthy deserted their sick relatives, the rich left everything behind, even the doctors fled out of fear. But the Christians stayed. Committed to caring for the sick, they remained in the city... and shocked the ancient world. One eyewitness, Dionysius of Alexandria, wrote:

Most of our Christian brothers and sisters showed unbounded love and loyalty, never sparing themselves and thinking only of one another. Heedless of danger, they took charge of the sick, attending to their every need and ministering to them in Christ...

The Romans had never seen anything like this. The world had never seen anything like it.

Over the past two thousand years, Jesus' call to care for the sick has changed the world. The very essence of healthcare and caring for the sick emerged through the Church, through the religious orders, in direct response to the value and dignity that the Gospel assigns to each and every human life.

While healthcare has been institutionalized, we are still called to continue this beautiful legacy of mercy by caring for the sick.

Even though we have hospitals, antibiotics, and intricate healthcare systems, we are still called to visit the sick. And not just the physically sick. Our age is also plagued by a mental health epidemic. Millions of men, women, and children are grappling with the overwhelming effects of anxiety, depression, and a wide range of other mental health conditions.

This Corporal Work of Mercy reflects the heart of the Gospel: to see Christ in the suffering of others, to bring hope where there is despair, and to comfort those who are in pain.

Whether you have a relative dying of cancer or a loved one going through a deep depression, we are called to Visit the Sick.

Living out this Corporal Work of Mercy to Visit the Sick requires both intentionality and compassion. It challenges us to go beyond our comfort zones and to prioritize the needs of others. There are so many simple practical ways to tend to the sick: offer to run errands, prepare a meal, sit with them, read to them, offer to take them to see their doctor, help with childcare, be an empathetic listener, or simply reach out to check in.

Each of these expressions of care and concern continue the vast tradition the early Christians set in motion. All these expressions of care and concern are practical manifestations of God's mercy. This faith in action is central to what it means to be a disciple of Jesus Christ.

It's not convenient. It may be uncomfortable at times. But Jesus' invitation to visit the sick asks us to go where others hesitate to go. This is one of the most powerful, countercultural impacts that the early Christians had on the world. . . and their impact lives on today in you and me.

The good we do never dies. It lives on, in other people, in other places, in other times.

Each Work of Mercy also draws us closer to Christ. Mercy is always an invitation to a better life, in large ways and small ways. Visiting the sick isn't just about helping others. It also transforms us. It teaches us humility. It fosters gratitude for our own health, which we often take for granted. It brings us face to face with the fragility of life. And it deepens our faith.

Jesus didn't see taking care of the sick as a side hustle, He didn't see it as an inconvenience, and He didn't see it as a distraction to His main mission. He exhibited a preference for those who were sick, whether their illness was physical or spiritual.

The Catechism reminds us of this enduring truth: *"Jesus' compassion toward all who suffer goes so far that he identifies himself with them: 'I was sick and you visited me.' His preferential love for the sick has not ceased through the centuries to draw the very special attention of Christians toward all those who suffer in body and soul. It is the source of tireless efforts to comfort them."* (CCC 1503) Inspired by this truth, Catholics care for more sick people every day than any other organization in the world.

Mercy is love reaching out to misery. Will you do your part?

Trust. Surrender. Believe. Receive.

LESSON

Jesus didn't see taking care of the sick as a side hustle, He didn't see it as an inconvenience, and He didn't see it as a distraction to His main mission. He exhibited a preference for those who were sick, whether their illness was physical or spiritual. The early Christians carried this on and captured the imagination of the whole world. Now it is your turn.

VIRTUE OF THE DAY

Attentiveness: The virtue of attentiveness is a sign of care for others and care for the soul, which is an immeasurable gift from God. Attentive people notice things, inside themselves, in the situations and circumstances of daily life, and in other people. They notice the person in the room who is suffering the most. Sustained attention in prayer is developed by practicing sustained attention in our work and with other people. Give the person in front of you in each moment your full attention.

DIVINE MERCY PRAYER

Eternal God, in whom mercy is endless and the treasury of compassion inexhaustible, look kindly upon us and increase Your mercy in us, that in difficult moments we might not despair nor become despondent, but with great confidence submit ourselves to Your holy will, which is Love and Mercy itself.

DAY 20
VISIT THE IMPRISONED

"Blessed are the merciful, for they will receive mercy." Matthew 5:7

A new prison was being built in Jonathan's small town. Everybody was talking about it, and nobody was happy. But for some reason Jonathan didn't feel that way.

It took two years to build the prison and Jonathan prayed every day for the prisoners that would be sent there. Some days he would drive to the building site on the outskirts of town and pray as he watched the builders laboring.

His wife didn't understand. His friends thought he was crazy. But Jonathan just kept hearing these words of Jesus: "I was in prison and you visited me." (Matthew 25:36) He wasn't a pastor, a counselor, or a social worker—just a regular person with a desire to make a difference.

"What do you want them to know?" his pastor asked him the Sunday before he first visited the prison. Jonathan replied, "I just want them to know they are more than their worst mistake."

Walking into the prison for the first time was an unsettling experience. The atmosphere was cold, the lighting was harsh, every sound—footsteps, the buzz of a security gate, or a distant shout—seemed amplified, adding to the tension, making the environment feel even more unwelcoming.

He was led to a room where a group of prisoners, dressed in orange jumpsuits, sat waiting for his visit. Jonathan was instantly seized by the concern that he wouldn't possibly be able to relate to them.

As he introduced himself, Jonathan shared a simple truth: "I'm here because I believe everyone deserves hope." His words seemed to hang in the air, met first with skepticism, then curiosity. A man who went by the name Raven finally broke the silence, "What makes you think we deserve hope?"

Jonathan didn't know what to say at first, but then he started to tell a story from his own life. He spoke of a time he'd felt trapped—not by bars, but by his own mistakes and regrets. He shared how someone had once reached out to him when he thought no one cared. "That small act of kindness changed everything for me," Jonathan said. "And I believe it can for you too."

The prisoners were skeptical, some thought they would never see him again. But week after week, Jonathan just kept showing up.

Over time, he became a familiar face at the prison. He listened to stories of loss and resilience, pain and transformation. Through weekly conversations, he learned that many of the men longed for forgiveness—both from others and from God, and like most of us, they were struggling to forgive themselves.

"All I have is my presence," he explained to his wife. "I just pray that my presence reminds them that they haven't been forgotten."

One day, Raven, the man who had first questioned Jonathan's intentions, shared something extraordinary, "You showing up every week has done something I never thought possible," he said. "It made me believe I'm more than my worst mistake."

When Raven was released after ten years, he stayed in touch with Jonathan. He found a job and began rebuilding his life. He even joined a program to mentor at-risk youth, using his own story to inspire others to make better choices.

Mercy is always an invitation to a better life, in large ways and small ways.

Visiting prisoners was a calling for Jonathan. It started as an act of service, but it became a lesson in what it means to be human. He learned that everyone, no matter their circumstances, carries within them the potential for change. By simply showing up, he offered something invaluable: the gift of presence.

This story is a reminder that small acts of kindness—like visiting someone who feels forgotten—can plant seeds of hope in ways you may never imagine.

When I wrote *33 Days to Eucharistic Glory*, I spent a lot of time reflecting on the power of the True Presence of Jesus in the Eucharist. There are two insights that come to mind in relation to mercy.

The first is that I have a true presence, a false presence, and a half presence. Being truly present to the person before us isn't easy. It requires real intentionality. The second is this: just as sitting in Jesus' presence is enough, often our own presence is enough for other people. They don't need us to say anything. They don't need us to fuss. Just being present is enough.

Jonathan's presence was enough for those prisoners. Your mere presence can be a great gift, not just to prisoners, but to anyone.

There are 1.9 million people incarcerated in the United States today. Our incarceration rate is 531 per 100,000 people. That's four times the incarceration rate of the United Kingdom (129 per 100,000), six times the incarceration rate of France (93 per 100,000), eight times the incarceration rate of Germany (67 per 100,000), and fourteen times the incarceration rate of Japan (37 per 100,000).

It is estimated that 5 percent of men and women in prison in the United States are innocent. If these estimates are correct, that would amount to fifty thousand people. I imagine it would be easy enough to lose hope in prison but imagine the anguish of sitting in a prison cell day and night for a crime you didn't commit. These people deserve our prayers and our advocacy.

There is however one thing I feel compelled to draw your attention to. It is getting harder to visit prisons for the purpose of ministry. And beyond that, there may be lots of factors that just make it impossible for you. That's okay. As we have discussed before, don't let what you can't do interfere with what you can do. And don't look away. Commit here and now, today, to live out this Corporal Work of Mercy in some way. Commit here and now, today, to visit the imprisoned with your prayers.

The Holy Spirit will help us find a way once we make the commitment. Love is creative. Let's ask the Holy Spirit to help us find creative ways to live out the Works of Mercy, just like Saint Vitalis did.

Twenty years ago, I knew a woman who was unable to leave her home due to a disability, but she was always talking about the Works of Mercy. Finally, one day, I asked her, "Elizabeth, you can't leave the home, how do you fulfill your commitment to the Works of Mercy?" She smiled and took me through them one by one, explaining the ways she had come up with to live them out with her disability. When it came to Visit the Imprisoned, Elizabeth explained she did research as a volunteer for two nonprofit organizations that work to exonerate people who have been wrongfully convicted and are serving prison sentences.

The one thing we can all do, the one way we can all visit the imprisoned, is with our prayers. We believe in the power of prayer, and the imprisoned desperately need our prayers. Let us visit them with our prayers each day. Add them to your morning prayers or your evening prayers, or to your prayer before meals.

There are also many ways to feel imprisoned in this world. Some people feel imprisoned by fear, anxiety, depression, a chronic illness, cultural expectations, a toxic relationship, poverty, debt, a job that is ill-suited for them, addiction, disability, and the list doesn't end there.

Mercy is love reaching out to misery. These people are experiencing a different form of imprisonment, but they also need us to be harbingers of hope. They too need God's grace and mercy to liberate them from their prisons.

Trust. Surrender. Believe. Receive.

LESSON

There are many ways to feel imprisoned in this world. Some people feel imprisoned by fear, anxiety, depression, a chronic illness, cultural expectations, a toxic relationship, poverty, debt, a job that is ill-suited for them, addiction, disability, and the list doesn't end there. And there are those who are physically imprisoned. We are each called to visit the imprisoned in some way. Your presence and your prayers are both powerful.

VIRTUE OF THE DAY
Boldness: The virtue of boldness is the willingness to act with confidence, courage, and determination in the face of difficulties, uncertainty, and opposition. It isn't recklessness or arrogance, but rather a measured steadfastness to do what is right, even when it is difficult or unpopular.

DIVINE MERCY PRAYER
Eternal God, in whom mercy is endless and the treasury of compassion inexhaustible, look kindly upon us and increase Your mercy in us, that in difficult moments we might not despair nor become despondent, but with great confidence submit ourselves to Your holy will, which is Love and Mercy itself.

DAY 21
BURY THE DEAD

"Blessed are the merciful, for they will receive mercy." Matthew 5:7

Burying the dead is a sacred and timeless act that is present in every culture and civilization. Burial practices and beliefs vary widely across cultures, reflecting unique perspectives on life, death, and the afterlife.

The Egyptians buried their pharaohs in pyramids full of food, drink, books, gold, furniture, jewelry, and anything they thought the pharaohs might need in the afterlife. Ordinary Egyptians were buried in the fetal position, which was a symbol of rebirth, and food, drink, and other material possessions were also placed in their graves.

Wealthy Vikings were buried in ships with weapons, treasures, and sometimes animals or slaves, believed to help them journey to Valhalla.

The Toraja people of Indonesia often kept the deceased in the home for months or years while families saved for elaborate funeral ceremonies.

In Tibet, bodies are left on mountaintops to be consumed by vultures, symbolizing the impermanence of life and the cycle of nature.

The Mayan people buried their dead with jade or corn in their mouths, symbolizing wealth or sustenance for the afterlife.

The Jewish people have a beautiful tradition known as "sitting *shiva*." The *shiva* period is the seven days of mourning that begin immediately after the burial. During these days, the immediate family of the deceased stays in their home, where their friends, family, and neighbors come together to support them, bringing food and solace.

As Catholics, our beliefs around burying the dead are rooted in the dignity of the human body, our faith in the Resurrection, and the hope for eternal life. The Catholic Church teaches that the human body is sacred because it is a temple of the Holy Spirit and a vessel of God's creation. We believe in the resurrection of the body. At the end of time, the body will be reunited with the soul and transformed into a glorified state.

Catholics believe in praying for the souls of the deceased, especially those in purgatory, to help purify them and hasten their entry into Heaven.

And it is especially important to note that our burial rituals include prayers imploring God to pour out His boundless mercy on the soul of the departed.

What happens when we die? The Catholic Church teaches, based on Scripture and Tradition, that when a person dies, their soul separates from their body, and experiences particular judgment by God where their eternal destiny is determined based on their faith and deeds during their earthly life. The options are Heaven, hell, and purgatory.

The Church teaches Heaven is for those who have lived a life of faith and virtue and are free from sin. Purgatory is for those who have died in a state of grace but still need purification for lesser sins or attachments. Hell is for those who have rejected God and died in a state of mortal sin.

Endless debate surrounds these matters, but some things are logical, rational, and beyond debate. For example, we believe that Heaven is eternal union with God. *"Heaven is the ultimate end and fulfillment of the deepest human longings, the state of supreme, definitive happiness."* (CCC 1024) Most people don't have much trouble believing in Heaven, but lots of people question the existence of purgatory. But if Heaven exists, purgatory must exist. If something impure is added to something that is pure it all becomes impure. If you take a single drop of motor oil and place it in a bottle of 100 percent pure virgin olive oil it is no longer pure olive oil.

The purification of purgatory is necessary because, as the Bible teaches, nothing impure can enter Heaven. (Revelation 21:27)

If this logic holds true, purgatory exists, and the people in purgatory need our prayers. This logic is also supported by the Scriptures: "It is a holy and wholesome thought to pray for the dead, that they may be loosed from sins." (2 Maccabees 12:45-46)

Every day we read and hear about famous people who have died. I always have the same thought: I wonder if he has anyone to pray for him? I wonder if she has anyone to pray for her? And then I find myself thrown into spontaneous prayer for that person's soul.

And as we discuss the Corporal Work of Mercy to Bury the Dead, I feel compelled to discuss something that I witness at too many funerals. People say things like, "Well, he is with God now," "She's in a better place," or "I'm sure he's up there with God looking down on us and smiling."

All these statements assume one thing: that the person we are burying is in Heaven with God.

This is a massive disservice to the people we love. Here's the problem: We don't pray for people in Heaven because people in Heaven don't need our prayers. But people in purgatory do need our prayers. So, if we assume someone is in Heaven who isn't in Heaven, it's unlikely we will pray for that person. And that is tragic.

I don't want anyone making that assumption when I die. I expect I will need a long stay in purgatory and I'm going to need all the prayers I can get.

An enormous part of burying the dead is praying for the dead, and they may need our prayers long after the day we lay them to rest. Mercy is always an invitation to a better life, in this life and the next.

Pray for your ancestors. When you hear someone has died, pray for them, especially those who may not have anyone to pray for them.

Mercy is love reaching out to misery. "Eternal rest grant unto them, O Lord, and may perpetual light shine upon them. May the souls of the faithful departed through the mercy of God rest in peace. Amen."

There are many ways to honor the dead. Attending a funeral is the most common. Each Work of Mercy benefits those we serve, but they also benefit us. Burying the dead prevents us from looking away from one of life's central facts: We are just pilgrims passing through this world. Each funeral leads us to examine our own lives. Death is a reminder to live life to the fullest.

Trust. Surrender. Believe. Receive.

LESSON
Burial is a sign of civilization. Christian burial is a sign of faith and a public declaration of hope. It is also an opportunity to share our grief and loss with the community, and to be supported and comforted by the Christian community.

VIRTUE OF THE DAY
Honor: The virtue of honor recognizes that every human being deserves respect because every human being is made in the image and likeness of God. Honor opens the way for phenomenal relationships and makes orderly community possible.

DIVINE MERCY PRAYER
Eternal God, in whom mercy is endless and the treasury of compassion inexhaustible, look kindly upon us and increase Your mercy in us, that in difficult moments we might not despair nor become despondent, but with great confidence submit ourselves to Your holy will, which is Love and Mercy itself.

DAY 22
INSTRUCT THE IGNORANT

"Blessed be God the Father of our Lord Jesus Christ! By his great mercy he has given us new life." 1 Peter 1:3

When I was fifteen years old and just beginning to take my faith seriously, I had a spiritual mentor who helped me build a spiritual life. We used to play basketball together. Each week he would ask me if I had any questions about the faith. I had so many questions. One by one he answered them.

What impressed me the most was what he did when he didn't know the answer to a question. "I don't know," he would say. "Let me look into it and I will get you the answer next week." The first time I remember thinking it was just a polite way to brush me off. But the following week he said, "I did some reading on your question from last week. This is the answer you were looking for..."

This open question forum was tremendously powerful in my spiritual development. But after a few months, I asked another question and he said, "It's time for you to go to the next level. It's time for you to learn how to find answers for yourself."

The year was 1988. Five years before the public had access to the Internet. So, the following week, I went to the library searching for answers to my latest questions in three books my mentor had recommended.

Those back-and-forth discussions around questions large and small had an enormous impact on my faith, and by extension, my life. That experience taught me so many lessons. Yes, I learned answers to a lot of questions I had about the Catholic faith. But I learned so much more. I learned how to find answers to questions. I developed the confidence to go looking for answers. I learned that it isn't good for us to have every answer served up to us on a silver platter. Searching for the answers to our questions builds character and expands our faith.

Most of all, I learned that there are answers to our questions, and the answers are beautiful. And I learned this: In order to see the beauty of the Catholic faith, in order to find answers to our deeply personal questions, our singular motive must be truth. You have to set aside your own agenda, whatever prejudices life has burdened you with so far, and the specific circumstances of your life. You have to prioritize the truth even if it condemns your own decisions and actions. Otherwise, we will remain deaf, dumb, and blind to the truth and beauty of God's ways.

The more I asked questions and the more I discovered answers, the more my confidence grew in the Catholic Church and her teachings. The questions not only led me to individual answers, but they allowed me to discover the coherent and comprehensive worldview that is Catholicism. Here I discovered that for two thousand years, the best Catholic minds have been gathering wisdom on every topic that touches on the human experience and that this gathered wisdom makes up an unimaginable treasure trove.

The First Spiritual Work of Mercy is Instruct the Ignorant.

In this story I was the ignorant and my spiritual mentor was the instructor. He accompanied me in my journey and that changed the whole trajectory of my life. He accompanied me in my journey, and I have been trying to do that for others ever since.

From the very first day in 2009, the masthead on DynamicCatholic.com has read: *Meeting people where they are... Leading them to where God calls them to be!* To accompany people in their faith journey is a crucial aspect of evangelization.

People deserve answers to their questions. This is one of my firmest convictions. It was born from this experience with my spiritual mentor. People deserve answers to their questions, especially questions surrounding the faith—not just generic, one-size-fits-all answers, but deeply personal answers that reach into their lives, meet them in their daily struggles, and deliver hope and clarity. They deserve answers that animate their lives in a uniquely Christian way. They need and deserve answers they can live.

This quest to help people find such answers is the quest to instruct the ignorant and an act of profound mercy.

We live in a time of moral and ethical confusion. We live in a time that is plagued by a crisis of purposelessness. Too many people have stopped thinking about the best way to live and have given themselves over to doing whatever they want. The invitation to instruct the ignorant has never been more relevant or more necessary.

People need clarity. Clarity is merciful.

There is genius in Catholicism. Catholicism is beautiful and unique in the clarity it provides. The Catholic Church has answers to questions. There will be times when we may not like those answers, but at those times we have usually deprioritized our quest for truth to justify our choices and actions.

The merciful thing to do is to share that clarity with as many people as possible. It's time to seek, find, live, and share the clarity and genius of Catholicism.

Some people may resist your efforts, but keep in mind, mercy is always an invitation to a better life.

Trust. Surrender. Believe. Receive.

LESSON

We live in a time of moral and ethical confusion. People need clarity. People deserve deeply personal answers to their deeply personal questions. It's an act of mercy to help them find those answers. Clarity is merciful.

VIRTUE OF THE DAY

Wisdom: The virtue of wisdom is the good judgment to consider the outcomes and consequences of today's choices on the future—in this life and in eternity. The world is drowning in information and knowledge but starving for wisdom. Wisdom is truth lived.

DIVINE MERCY PRAYER

Eternal God, in whom mercy is endless and the treasury of compassion inexhaustible, look kindly upon us and increase Your mercy in us, that in difficult moments we might not despair nor become despondent, but with great confidence submit ourselves to Your holy will, which is Love and Mercy itself.

DAY 23
COUNSEL THE DOUBTFUL

"Blessed be God the Father of our Lord Jesus Christ! By his great mercy he has given us new life." 1 Peter 1:3

Do your doubts unsettle you, or do you see them as an invitation to grow?

Doubts are a natural component of our spiritual journey. When doubts arise in your heart, don't see them as failures or threats to your faith. See them as opportunities to grow in faith. Faith and doubt go hand in hand, and often, the greater the faith, the greater the doubts. Our doubts can be a great antagonist in our faith story. This antagonist often draws us into a deeper experience of faith as long as we remain in pursuit of truth and don't begin to pursue an excuse.

The most famous doubter in history is of course Thomas. Poor Thomas. He might have just been having a bad day. Yet this one situation has defined him throughout history as the great doubter, referred to as Doubting Thomas more often than as Saint Thomas. Do you know anything else about Thomas? Many people know only that Jesus appeared to the disciples when Thomas was out running errands and he didn't believe them. (John 20:24-29)

The stunning example in our own times is that of Mother Teresa. Declared by many a saint during her lifetime, and by the Church less than twenty years after her death, she was a light of faith and hope in the world. Yet after her death her private papers revealed that she had suffered from incredible doubt, and for long periods of her life she felt that God was absent. Using words like "darkness," "dryness," "torture," and "loneliness," she wrote about the spiritual agony she often experienced, comparing it to hell and revealing that at one time her doubts were so great that she even questioned the existence of God.

These were astounding but important revelations. Too often we have left these types of things out when telling the stories of the saints. This is a massive disservice to ordinary people like you and me, struggling to live our faith each day amid our doubts and limitations. Authentic faith is going to have to wrestle with doubt from time to time. It's important not to lose sight of the fact that this is natural, normal, and healthy.

Thomas was skeptical, but he was open to the truth. Some people use their doubts to lead them to answers, others use their doubts as an excuse to opt out of humanity's epic search for truth. Blaise Pascal wrote, "In faith there is enough light for those who want to believe and enough shadows to blind those who don't."

It is natural to have doubts, but we have a responsibility to seek out the truth that will assuage our doubts. Seeking answers to our personal questions and wrestling with our doubts helps us to build a more robust faith.

The Second Spiritual Work of Mercy—Counsel the Doubtful—involves helping other people to work through their doubts.

Doubts are flawed because they can never be fully satisfied. They demand proof, but they question any proof that is offered. There is no proof, evidence, or answer that will ever satisfy some doubts. There would be no need for faith if proof was available.

Healthy faith asks questions. The important thing is to stay focused on your search for truth. Examine your motives: Are you looking for answers or are you looking for an excuse not to believe? The former will grow your faith; the latter will destroy it. Investigate your doubts by all means, but do it with a hunger for truth.

I'll be the first to admit that I have doubts from time to time. Some pass away in a day. Others cling to my mind and heart for long stretches. It's these longer-lasting doubts that challenge my perspective and invite me to grow in trust. What are your doubts?

How might God be inviting you to trust Him more because of those doubts, not in spite of them?

We all need people in our lives we can trust to give us wise advice, to provide a new perspective, to encourage us to find the way forward when we are lost, and to counsel us in our doubts. You need this and everyone in your life—your children, your spouse, your friends, your family—has this need too.

Counsel the Doubtful. This Work of Mercy asks us to meet people where they are in their doubt with compassion and patience. It's a call to help them see their doubts as an invitation to greater faith. The definition of "counsel" is "to advise" and "to recommend a course of action." Yet, far too often, our impulse is to judge or even rebuke those who reveal their doubts.

There are three fundamental shifts we can make that will empower us to effectively counsel the doubtful.

The first is to get comfortable with uncertainty. In matters of faith, certainty is a myth; one of the essential requirements of faith is the absence of certainty. If you can be certain, there is no need for faith. And yet the demand for proof and certainty has become one of the idols of our age, an idol that has separated millions from God. The more comfortable we become with uncertainty in our own lives, the more capable we are of helping others make peace with their own uncertainty. This is essential to counseling others in their doubts.

The second crucial shift is to banish judgment from our hearts. This begins with avoiding the poison of judging yourself. Don't judge your doubts. Remember, great faith and great doubt go hand in hand. Even the saints were plagued by doubt at times. It's what they did with their doubts that made all the difference. Learn to see your doubts as an invitation to greater faith and you will be far less inclined to judge others for their doubts. Instead, you'll be equipped to help them see their doubts as an invitation to grow in their faith.

Counseling the doubtful is a powerful act of mercy. Some people may resist your efforts, but keep in mind, mercy is always an invitation to a better life.

The third fundamental shift is from self-reliance to asking God to do what only God can do. Yes, we should study the Scriptures, read great books about the faith, and immerse ourselves in spiritual practices. And still, it is vital that we keep in mind that faith is a gift. Faith, Hope, and Charity—the three theological virtues—are infused in our souls by God. Only God can give us faith. So, let's ask.

Counseling the doubtful also involves teaching people to pray for faith. I offer you this prayer as a way to practically accompany your doubts.

When your heart is troubled by doubts, pray this short prayer over and over throughout the day: *"Lord, increase my faith."* Pray it dozens of times a day.

Trust. Surrender. Believe. Receive.

LESSON

Faith and doubt go hand in hand, and often, the greater the faith, the greater the doubt. Our doubts can be a great antagonist in our faith story. This antagonist often draws us into a deeper experience of faith as long as we remain in pursuit of truth and don't begin to pursue an excuse.

VIRTUE OF THE DAY

Prudence: The virtue of prudence gives you the ability to discern what is good, true, right, just, and lasting. Prudence enables you to exercise foresight and good judgment, establish the right priorities in your life, and make wise decisions, while considering all potential consequences.

DIVINE MERCY PRAYER

Eternal God, in whom mercy is endless and the treasury of compassion inexhaustible, look kindly upon us and increase Your mercy in us, that in difficult moments we might not despair nor become despondent, but with great confidence submit ourselves to Your holy will, which is Love and Mercy itself.

DAY 24
ADMONISH THE SINNER

"Blessed be God the Father of our Lord Jesus Christ! By his great mercy he has given us new life." 1 Peter 1:3

How is the best way to live?

The best way to live is one of life's biggest questions. This is the question that the great thinkers of every age grapple with. It is also a question that we each wrestle with in a deeply personal way. We are all searching for the best way to live. Sometimes it is a conscious search and sometimes it is an unconscious yearning for something more or different. But it's a question we must each answer for ourselves.

I have come to the conclusion that the Gospel of Jesus Christ is the best way to live. I have thought long and hard about this, explored dozens of philosophies, and foolishly tried to come up with my own self-interested way of living, but all of these fell short.

I am totally convinced that the life Jesus invites us to in the Gospels is the best way to live. In fact, I am so convinced that even if you could prove to me that God does not exist, that eternity does not exist, and that we simply cease to exist after we die, I would still believe that the teachings of Jesus offer the best way to live.

I am a practical man. The Gospel works. It helps everyone who embraces it to increasingly become more perfectly themselves.

It celebrates the dignity of the human person, which is a primary truth that is indispensable if we are to understand the world around us. It fosters phenomenal relationships and encourages vibrant and orderly community. It promotes right relationships between humanity and nature. It just works. In an amazingly practical way, the Gospel is the answer to all the deeply personal questions of life and the light that shows us the next step to take in our journey.

There is simply no better way to live. And the joy! The joy that comes from living the teachings of Jesus Christ is unmistakable. Nothing else brings such joy.

The Third Spiritual Work of Mercy—Admonish the Sinner—is about encouraging others in the direction of that joy.

The word *admonish* comes from the Latin word *admonere*, meaning to remind or advise. Admonishing the sinner isn't a call to judge, reprimand, or control people. It's an invitation to remind others that there is a "best way to live." To admonish the sinner is to say, "You are making yourself miserable by looking for joy in the wrong place."

We all need to be rescued from the error of our ways. We all need to be saved from our self-destructive beliefs and behaviors. These errors are a form of misery, and mercy is love reaching out to misery. It is always an invitation to a better life.

There is a reality that we don't like to talk about. You can mis-live your life. Most people never consider it as a possibility, but it's true. You can mis-live your life. We assume that all lives are well-lived. It isn't true. We deceive ourselves.

The disturbing truth is you don't even need to do something significantly egregious. You don't need to become a drug addict or murder someone to mis-live your life. You can do it in the most mundane and ordinary ways. It can happen so subtly that the people around you wouldn't even notice, because you have most likely surrounded yourself with people mis-living their lives in exactly the same ways.

All it takes is the consistent application of mediocrity, laziness, procrastination, obsession with material possessions, and self-centeredness.

This is why we need to be admonished. This is why we are called to admonish others.

Think of a time in your past when you were headed down a dark and self-destructive path. Maybe you were in a toxic relationship. Perhaps you were stuck in a soul-crushing job. Maybe you were caught up in a cycle of bad financial decisions or running with friends who brought out the worst in you. Maybe you were ignoring your health or burying your talents. Thinking about having an affair, getting carried away by an addiction, ego getting out of control, gossip becoming central to your conversations... There are plenty of times in our lives when we need a true friend who cares more about the eternal destination of our soul than anything else. We need someone who is willing to go out on a limb to admonish us.

Some people will thank you for it, others will hate you for it. I'm not going to pretend otherwise, but their reaction doesn't matter. Your words will keep stirring their hearts long after you speak them, and a week from now or three years from now, they may wake up and respond to your reminder.

These reminders are a great mercy, because the uncomfortable truth is it is possible to mis-live our lives and the stakes are huge.

When God challenges us to change our lives, we may resist at first, but keep in mind, mercy is always an invitation to a better life.

It is also helpful to examine how we respond to correction, coaching, reminders, and warnings. How coachable are you?

Champions love coaching. They are so committed to excellence that they would listen to their worst enemy's advice if it would help them run half a second faster (or the equivalent in their particular sport or discipline). Their desire for excellence in their sport often dwarfs our desire for spiritual excellence.

We have perhaps all become too comfortable with our spiritual mediocrity. But if someone knew a better way, a way that led to fulfilment and happiness, wouldn't you want them to tell you?

Sometimes we need a reminder that we are in danger of mis-living our lives. There are people in your life who will remind you from time to time. Those people are a merciful blessing. There are people in your life who *need* you to remind them, too. These are difficult conversations. It's natural to be anxious and fearful. Courage comes from remembering there's simply too much at stake to stay silent.

Trust. Surrender. Believe. Receive.

LESSON

The word *admonish* comes from the Latin word *admonere*, meaning to remind or advise. Admonishing the sinner isn't a call to judge, reprimand, or control people. It's an invitation to remind others that there is a "best way to live." To admonish the sinner is to say, "You are making yourself miserable by looking for joy in the wrong place." It is always an invitation to a better life.

VIRTUE OF THE DAY

Sincerity: The virtue of sincerity involves being free from pretense, deceit, and hypocrisy. It is achieved by governing our words and actions with truth and justice. Keep your promises. If you say you will do something, do it.

DIVINE MERCY PRAYER

Eternal God, in whom mercy is endless and the treasury of compassion inexhaustible, look kindly upon us and increase Your mercy in us, that in difficult moments we might not despair nor become despondent, but with great confidence submit ourselves to Your holy will, which is Love and Mercy itself.

DAY 25
BEAR WRONGS PATIENTLY

"Blessed be God the Father of our Lord Jesus Christ! By his great mercy he has given us new life." 1 Peter 1:3

People are going to hurt you. It's an uncomfortable truth, but a truth, nonetheless. Sometimes people wrong us intentionally. At other times, it's the result of their brokenness, or a misunderstanding, or carelessness. These offenses can range from cutting you off in traffic and saying something sarcastic to someone lying about you, stealing from you, cheating on you, constantly criticizing you, and worse.

The question is: How will you respond next time someone hurts you?

The Fourth Spiritual Work of Mercy is Bear Wrongs Patiently.

What does that mean? To bear wrongs patiently means to endure injustices, offenses, or hurt gracefully, without succumbing to anger, bitterness, or the desire for revenge. It is about choosing to respond in a way that reflects the mercy of God when someone wrongs us.

Jesus models this behavior over and over throughout His life. I cannot even begin to imagine the patience Jesus needed to put up with the nonsense of people every day of life.

If we asked one thousand people on the street to name the ten most important moments in history, lots of people wouldn't mention Jesus. Answers would include: The Agricultural Revolution, the Shang Dynasty, the invention of writing, the Silk Road, the rise and fall of Constantinople, the rise and fall of the Roman Empire, the invention of the printing press, the signing of the Declaration of Independence, the Industrial Revolution, the invention of the automobile, the first antibiotic, World War II, landing on the moon, the invention of the computer, the Civil Rights Movement, the fall of the Berlin Wall, the Great Depression, or the birth of the Internet.

These are all significant moments, indeed pivotal in our history, but I would argue that all ten of the most important moments in history are found in the life of Jesus Christ. We could start with the birth, death, and Resurrection of Jesus, move on to the Last Supper, and continue from there. But the reality is, if Jesus is who He says He is, any moment of His life was more important than the invention of anything.

The Sermon on the Mount was also one of the most significant moments in history. These teachings of Jesus have profoundly influenced the way human beings have lived since He walked the earth. His emphasis on love, mercy, justice, and the dignity of every individual has left an enduring mark on our understanding of morality and human rights. This single collection of teachings redefined our entire understanding of what it means to be a human being and live in relationship with others and as members of society. These teachings reveal the heart of God and invite us to experience and share His mercy.

The Sermon on the Mount is found in The Gospel of Matthew, chapters five through seven. Most people can read it in less than thirty minutes, and I encourage you to read it in one sitting. And though it may take less than thirty minutes to read, to fully understand even one of the teachings it contains can take a lifetime.

Reflecting on the Sermon on the Mount is a powerful way to learn and absorb the wisdom of Divine Mercy. It will teach you more about Divine Mercy than all the books written on the subject, including this one.

So, let's explore what it teaches us about bearing wrongs patiently.

"You have heard that it was said, 'An eye for an eye and a tooth for a tooth.' But I say to you, Do not resist one who is evil. But if any one strikes you on the right cheek, turn to him the other also; and if any one would sue you and take your coat, let him have your cloak as well; and if any one forces you to go one mile, go with him two miles. Give to him who begs from you, and do not refuse him who would borrow from you." (Matthew 5:38-42)

This was a radical teaching two thousand years ago, and like all of Jesus' teachings, it is still a radical teaching today. It didn't get any easier over the past two thousand years to love your enemy, trust in God, forgive without limits, resist the temptation to judge other people, detach from material possessions, deny yourself, or carry your cross.

But this particular teaching completely revolutionized human morality. Jesus was throwing out the "eye for an eye and a tooth for a tooth" mentality, and yet we are still clinging to it today. He was also saying: Stop stealing from God.

Did I lose you? The Scriptures teach us, "'Vengeance is mine,' says the Lord." (Deuteronomy 32:35 and Romans 12:19) The eye for an eye and a tooth for a tooth mentality claims vengeance as a human right and Jesus was reminding people that it isn't.

So, when someone wrongs you, you have two choices: Bear the wrong patiently or steal from God. It is humbling to admit that I still find myself stealing from God far too often. This teaching is constantly challenging me to rearrange my priorities and change my behavior.

When someone wrongs you, how do you react? The last time someone cut you off in traffic, what did you think or say about them? When you find out someone has been gossiping about you, how do you respond? Our minds almost always wander in the direction of vengeance. Our minds start dreaming up ways to get them back. And perhaps you have been wronged in much more serious ways. Perhaps someone betrayed you in a way that has shaken you to your very core. What was your first impulse? Revenge or healing?

We are all broken and wounded. Our hearts aren't inclined to bear wrongs patiently or to forgive offenses willingly. This requires virtue.

Left to our own devices, humans are vengeful. Even a cursory examination of human history will prove this beyond a doubt. Christianity proposes to change this, and the change is possible because of Jesus' radical example.

We are not naturally kind and merciful, slow to anger, and rich in compassion. These attitudes and behaviors are learned as we seek to walk in God's ways by living a life of virtue.

How should we respond to those who wrong us? This question is central to the life of every Christian. Jesus doesn't just speak the answer. He lives the answer. Unjustly condemned, stripped of His clothes and dignity, spat on, scourged, wearing a crown of thorns, He never lashes out. He has the power to make it all stop, and yet, He hangs on the Cross and says, "Father, forgive them for they know not what they do."

Is it easy to be a Pilgrim of Mercy? Absolutely not. Bearing wrongs patiently takes practice. Don't worry. The people in your life will give you plenty of opportunities to practice it each day. The next time someone wrongs you, pause to pray. Ask for the patience to respond with love and mercy, rather than impatiently reacting with anger or hate. Remind yourself that you have wronged others in the past, intentionally and unintentionally, and that even with your best efforts to avoid it, you will wrong people in the future.

Mercy is always an invitation to a better life. A Pilgrim of Mercy turns the other cheek and extends that invitation even to those who have wronged them.

Trust. Surrender. Believe. Receive.

LESSON
People are going to hurt you. It's an uncomfortable truth, but a truth, nonetheless. Sometimes people wrong us intentionally. At other times, it's the result of their brokenness, or a misunderstanding, or carelessness. A Pilgrim of Mercy endures injustices, offenses, or hurt gracefully, without succumbing to anger, bitterness, or the desire for revenge. It is about choosing to respond in a way that reflects the mercy of God.

VIRTUE OF THE DAY
Patience: The virtue of patience deepens your ability to meet life's challenges. It is a form of mild suffering that refines character. Discipline yourself to be patient many times each day. It is a spiritual investment that will pay great dividends. Saint Teresa of Ávila had a bookmark upon which she had written, "This too shall pass." Patience is simply allowing it to pass.

DIVINE MERCY PRAYER
Eternal God, in whom mercy is endless and the treasury of compassion inexhaustible, look kindly upon us and increase Your mercy in us, that in difficult moments we might not despair nor become despondent, but with great confidence submit ourselves to Your holy will, which is Love and Mercy itself.

DAY 26
FORGIVE OFFENSES WILLINGLY

"Blessed be God the Father of our Lord Jesus Christ! By his great mercy he has given us new life." 1 Peter 1:3

There can be no peace without forgiveness.

Forgiveness is one of the central lessons in the life and teachings of Jesus. It plays a powerful role in the spiritual health of every person. It also plays a powerful role in every relationship, and it is essential to the life of any healthy community, whether that community is as small as a family or as large as a nation. It is also essential to giving and receiving Divine Mercy.

When we forgive, we share the love of God with others and rid ourselves of dangerous poisons that can prevent us from growing spiritually. The benefits are clear, but that doesn't make it easy.

Who is my neighbor? may be the most important question when it comes to human relations, but very close behind it is the question: *How many times do I have to forgive my neighbor?*

"Peter came to Jesus and asked, 'How many times shall I forgive a brother or sister who has sinned against me? As many as seven times?' Jesus said to him, 'Not seven times, but seventy-seven times.'" (Matthew 18:21-22)

Without forgiveness our souls begin to fill with anger, resentment, frustration, and anxiety. Choosing not to forgive someone is like drinking poison and expecting the other person to die. When we choose not to forgive, we turn our backs on God and abandon the-best-version-of-ourselves.

Everybody needs to forgive somebody. Whom do you need to forgive? Whom is God inviting you to forgive?

Forgiveness is also a powerful countercultural element of Christianity. While Jesus' teaching about forgiveness was and is radical, He calls us beyond forgiveness. One of His most radical teachings is: "Love your enemies and pray for those who persecute you." (Matthew 5:44) What was the teaching before Jesus wandered into the synagogue that morning? "An eye for an eye, and a tooth for a tooth." (Exodus 21:24)

We spoke about it yesterday. We may have heard this reading many times. But the moment Jesus proclaimed this teaching was actually one of the great moral, ethical, and spiritual advances in human history. Jesus spiritually outlawed revenge and vengeance with one sentence.

What is He saying? He is saying love Emperor Nero, Adolf Hitler, Osama bin Laden, and child molesters, and pray for them. This teaching is so radical that when we really stop to think about it, our chests get tight, the airways to our lungs become constricted, and we find it hard to breathe.

Who are your enemies? When was the last time you prayed for them? There are some people who say they don't have any enemies. They simply have not thought it through. Who are the people on television who make your skin crawl and your blood boil? Who are the people who represent ideas that are at the other end of the ideological spectrum from everything that you hold to be good, true, noble, and just? These people are your enemies. When was the last time you prayed for them?

Radical, huh? And let's not forget the everyday ways people wrong you. They steal your parking spot, jump in front of you to get through the express lane at the supermarket, or say things about you that are not true.

Forgiveness is one of the most radical challenges Jesus levels at us. It is at once incredibly spiritual and monumentally practical. Our willingness to forgive and be forgiven often reveals the depth, or limitations, of our Christianity.

Forgiveness is one of most powerful and practical expressions of Divine Mercy we can participate in. But how?

Many years ago, a priest gave a homily on forgiveness that I'll never forget. The priest invited us to call to mind one person that we were having trouble forgiving. He then led us through the *Our Father*, but with a fresh twist. He told us that when we came to the line "forgive us our trespasses, as we forgive those who trespass against us," we were to lift that person up to God in our hearts.

I invite you to try this exercise with me now. Think of that person you struggle to forgive. Name them in your heart. Whisper their name out loud if you are alone. Name the way they hurt you. Now, keep them in your mind as we pray together:

Our Father, who art in heaven,
hallowed be Thy name;
Thy kingdom come;
Thy will be done
on earth as it is in heaven.
Give us this day our daily bread;
and forgive us our trespasses
as we forgive those who trespass against us;
and lead us not into temptation,
but deliver us from evil.
Amen.

Mercy is always an invitation to a better life.
Trust. Surrender. Believe. Receive.

LESSON

There can be no peace without forgiveness. When we forgive, we share the love of God with others and rid ourselves of dangerous poisons that can prevent us from growing spiritually. Without forgiveness our souls begin to fill with anger, resentment, frustration, and anxiety. Choosing not to forgive someone is like drinking poison and expecting the other person to die.

VIRTUE OF THE DAY

Forgiveness: The virtue of forgiveness is to willingly set aside any anger, resentment, or bitterness toward someone who has wronged you, been unfair or hurtful, or harmed you in any way. It is not about excusing sinful behavior or pretending we have not been harmed, but rather, it is about releasing bitterness and leaving judgement to God. By pardoning those who wrong us, we reflect the grace and mercy of God.

DIVINE MERCY PRAYER

Eternal God, in whom mercy is endless and the treasury of compassion inexhaustible, look kindly upon us and increase Your mercy in us, that in difficult moments we might not despair nor become despondent, but with great confidence submit ourselves to Your holy will, which is Love and Mercy itself.

DAY 27
COMFORT THE AFFLICTED

"Blessed be God the Father of our Lord Jesus Christ! By his great mercy he has given us new life." 1 Peter 1:3

Everyone you will ever meet is carrying a heavy burden. Everyone. Everyone is fighting a hard battle and, in some way, just living from day to day.

The Sixth Spiritual Work of Mercy is Comfort the Afflicted.

Life is difficult. Not for some people, but for everyone in their own way. And for far too many people, the world is a sad, unjust, brutal, randomly cruel, and maddening place. But people don't walk around with a sign around their neck that announces what they are struggling with.

"I'm depressed."

"Yesterday I had a miscarriage."

"I lost my job two weeks ago, but don't know how to tell my wife."

"My husband just told me he doesn't love me anymore."

"Am I a good mother?"

"I'm addicted to drugs."

"I want to break off my engagement."

"I don't know what to do with my life."

"My son won't talk to me."

"I just found out I have cancer."

People don't walk around with signs. But everyone's struggling with something. When we are mindful of this, we are gentler with each other. When we forget this, we abandon our humanity. Everyone you will ever meet is fighting a hard battle, even if it doesn't seem like it. We measure other people's lives by their blessings, but we don't see their hidden burdens. You never know what is going on inside somebody—and everyone has something going on inside them.

Even Jesus. One of the most heart-wrenching scenes in Jesus' life unfolded the night before He died. Knowing that He was about to take on the entire weight of humanity's brokenness, Jesus was afflicted with terrible pain and anxiety. In the Garden of Gethsemane, His pain was so great that He confided in His disciples, saying: "My soul is very sorrowful, even to death. Remain here and watch with me." (Matthew 26:38)

When Jesus was in the depth of His stress, anxiety, and anguish, He only requested one thing: company. He just wanted the people He loved the most to be by His side. He wanted to be comforted in His affliction.

When we see people suffering affliction, we don't always know what to do. But Jesus makes it clear: We don't have to say the perfect thing or do the perfect thing to comfort someone in their most difficult moments. Sometimes it's enough just to be there. Our presence is powerful.

Our presence says: "I see you. I hear you. You are worthy. I am with you. I care. Rest a while. You are safe here with me."

Every person you meet is fighting a hard battle. It might be obvious. It might be completely and utterly hidden. But let's start paying attention.

Look at the people you encounter today. Really look at them. See them. Most people feel unseen. Listen to the people you encounter today. Really listen to them. Hear them. Most people feel unheard. Go above and beyond to understand the people you encounter today. Seek to understand their perspective and whatever it is they are struggling with. Understand their plight. Most people feel misunderstood. Pay attention to the people in your life. These are very practical ways to bring the mercy and comfort of God to others.

Mercy is simple, beautiful, and practical.

Trust. Surrender. Believe. Receive.

LESSON

Make an effort to really look at, listen to, and understand the people you encounter today. Comforting the afflicted doesn't mean taking away their suffering. Sometimes it simply means acknowledging their suffering and accompanying them as they carry their cross.

VIRTUE OF THE DAY

Calmness: The virtue of calmness is the ability to remain composed and peaceful, even during difficult situations, which allows clear thinking and wise decision making.

DIVINE MERCY PRAYER

Eternal God, in whom mercy is endless and the treasury of compassion inexhaustible, look kindly upon us and increase Your mercy in us, that in difficult moments we might not despair nor

become despondent, but with great confidence submit ourselves to Your holy will, which is Love and Mercy itself.

DAY 28
PRAY FOR THE LIVING AND THE DEAD

"Blessed be God the Father of our Lord Jesus Christ! By his great mercy he has given us new life." 1 Peter 1:3

GOD ISN'T FIXING THIS.

That was the headline in the *New York Daily News*. It was emblazoned in huge white letters on the black cover of the magazine. Scattered around the cover were pictures of tweets offering "thoughts and prayers" for the victims of the latest mass shooting on American soil, which tragically left fourteen dead in San Bernardino, California.

"Our thoughts and prayers are with you." This phrase is a part of our culture. First used by Queen Elizabeth II, Harry Truman, and Dwight Eisenhower in the middle of the twentieth century, it has been used in response to all types of calamities from natural disasters to terrorist attacks.

For seventy-five years it has been customary for leaders of all types to express a promise of "thoughts and prayers" and with the emergence of social media it has become customary for ordinary people from all walks of life to post, "Our thoughts and prayers are with you."

But now something else has become all too common. Understandably frustrated that these tragedies continue to occur, some people spend their time and energy denouncing and ridiculing the power of prayer. This type of criticism has come to be called "prayer-shaming."

Here are just a few examples of these types of messages in the wake of recent tragedies:

"They were in church. They had the prayers shot right out of them. Maybe try something else."

"Dear 'thoughts and prayers' people: Please shut up and slink away. You are the problem, and everyone knows it."

"Prayer: How to do nothing and still think you're helping."

"Ooooooh. It's prayers and condolences now!? Well, that's WAY better than #thoughtsandprayers followed by zero action."

"#ThoughtsAndPrayers aren't enough."

First, it is important to acknowledge that the desire these messages convey for decisive action to prevent more tragedy is a good desire. As we hear in the Letter of Saint James, "Faith by itself, if it has no works, is dead." (James 2:17) Pope Francis once put it this way: "Prayer that doesn't lead to concrete action toward our brothers is a fruitless and incomplete prayer." Offering our "thoughts and prayers" does risk becoming a mere platitude if we don't pair it with love for our neighbors. And it certainly has no value if we simply tweet it out but never actually enter the classroom of silence to pray as we have promised.

These messages also reveal the spiritual poverty of our culture. Extreme secularism banishes God and denies the need to feed the human soul. A person who is praying is therefore seen as doing nothing. Worse yet, that person is ridiculed and shamed for their prayer, because some have decided prayer is unproductive and useless.

Whether we realize it or not in the moment, these comments are diametrically opposed to Christianity. Throughout the Gospels we hear that Jesus went away to a quiet place to pray.

Was Jesus wasting His time?

I think not. Our culture is desperately in need of prayer and reflection. The meaning and purpose we hunger for will never be found by excluding spirituality.

I honestly don't know how people live without prayer. I can tell the difference in myself on days when I don't pray. I'm less patient and more anxious, I give people the benefit of the doubt less and judge more, I think about myself more and I'm less generous with others, and the list goes on and on. I know for certain that prayer makes me a better friend, husband, father, brother, son, employer, and citizen.

It is possible to mis-live our lives and our chances increase exponentially if we neglect prayer and reflection.

In the summer of 1845, Henry David Thoreau left Concord, Massachusetts, because he believed it had become too busy, too noisy, too distracting. He built himself a little hut out by Walden Pond and began a two-year experiment in simplicity. During his time in the woods, he wrote these words:

"I went to the woods because I wanted to live deliberately. . . I wanted to live deep and suck out all the marrow of life . . . to put to rout all that was not life. . . and not, when I came to die, discover that I had not lived."

He has captured here some compelling reasons to pray. I go to the woods of prayer each day because I want to live life deliberately. I pray because I want to live life deeply and suck out all the marrow of life! I pray because I want to figure out what matters most and what is of little or no consequence. I pray because I do not want to come to die and discover that I have not lived.

I have tried life with and without prayer. With prayer is better. Life without prayer is unbearable. Without prayer, life doesn't make sense. I don't know how people live without prayer. I don't know how someone could remain sane in this crazy, noisy, busy world without a few minutes in the classroom of silence each day.

But I understand why people don't pray. I see how it happens. Many have never been taught how to simply be with God, and the sheer busyness of our lives can be overwhelming.

The spiritual poverty of our age is robbing us of the benefits of prayer. But it's also robbing everyone in our life of those benefits, and it's robbing everyone in our family trees.

The Seventh Spiritual Work of Mercy is Pray for the Living and the Dead. Every family in every generation needs a prayerful giant to cover their family in prayer.

Would you steal from a dead person? Most people would consider it a profound moral failure to steal from the dead. To paint a clearer picture, if there was a dead man on the sidewalk and someone came up and stole his wallet and his watch, how would you regard that person?

To deny the power of prayer is to steal from the dead, because the denial ultimately leads less people to pray for their dead relatives and friends. When we slip into the secular belief that prayer is useless, we also deny those we love most in this world the power of our prayers.

When was the last time you really prayed for someone? I mean every day by name and for specific intentions. That kind of prayer is powerful. I have been covered in that type of prayer and I know firsthand how very powerful it is. Give someone that gift. And tell them you are praying for them by name every day.

I have known the power of this prayer. Tony and Lorraine Grace were youth group leaders in my parish while I was growing up in Australia. "We are praying for you by name every day." They told me this every time they saw me. They explained that they did morning prayer together each day and then prayed for a list of people, one at a time, each by name. That's commitment. That's consistency. They were prayerful giants.

So many people have prayed for me and this ministry, and their prayers have been the source of great strength and comfort. There have been so many dark moments of discouragement in ministry over the years, and this darkness is usually experienced when you are far from the love and support of family and friends.

The world says that prayer is useless, but your prayers can have a profound influence on other people and the outcome of events.

The world needs a new generation of the people of God who are prepared to abandon the materialism and secularism of these modern times. Men and women who know the value of a soul in the context of now and eternity. Men and women who are able to raise their eyes from the things of this world to the greater things of the next world. People who allow Heaven and earth to meet each day in their prayer and in every activity of their lives. Will you be one of them?

Mercy is always an invitation to a better life. Are you ready to embrace that better life?

Trust. Surrender. Believe. Receive.

LESSON

Prayer is essential to the human experience. The spiritual poverty of our age is robbing us of the benefits of prayer. But it is also robbing everyone in our life of those benefits, and it is robbing our family trees, past and present. Your prayers can have a profound influence.

VIRTUE OF THE DAY

Consistency: The virtue of consistency allows us to moderate our behavior in alignment with our faith and values. It requires us to abandon frivolous whims, preferences, and cravings as they arise throughout the day and stay true to the course we have set. It also requires constant micro-alignments between our words, beliefs, and actions. Consistent people are sometimes mistaken for being boring, but only by those who don't value the rare peace consistency ushers quietly into our lives.

DIVINE MERCY PRAYER

Eternal God, in whom mercy is endless and the treasury of compassion inexhaustible, look kindly upon us and increase Your mercy in us, that in difficult moments we might not despair nor become despondent, but with great confidence submit ourselves to Your holy will, which is Love and Mercy itself.

DAY 29
WHAT IF?

"The Lord is kind and merciful, slow to anger and abounding in steadfast love." Psalm 103:8

What if everything the Catholic Church teaches is true? Have you ever paused to consider that possibility? Not just for a fleeting moment, but really taken some time to ponder the possibility. We live in a culture that assumes that the Church's teachings are false, unrealistic, or bigoted. It's time we seriously considered the other possibility. Because if it is all true—if everything the Catholic Church teaches is true—that changes everything.

What if God really does exist and created you out of love, for a purpose and with a mission that only you can fulfill? What if Jesus Christ really did come into the world, suffer, die, and rise again to save you? What if every Mass is a miraculous encounter where bread and wine become the Body and Blood of Christ to nourish your soul and draw you closer to eternity with God?

If everything the Catholic Church teaches is true, then your life is far more extraordinary than you could ever imagine. You're not a random accident. You're a child of God, called to greatness, created for eternity. Every choice you make, every act of love, every moment of prayer matters—infinitely and forever.

What if the Catholic Church's teachings on the dignity of every human person, the sanctity of marriage, and the importance of forgiveness are not just ideals but divine truths? What if the sacraments are not merely ancient rituals but deeply personal encounters with God's grace that can heal you, transform you, and guide you through life? What if Heaven is real and you are destined for it?

If all of this is true, how you live your life matters. It means we are called to something greater than pleasure, comfort, and worldly accomplishment. It means our faith is not just one part of our lives but the very foundation of everything.

And what if you lived as though it were all true? What if you prayed with the confidence that God hears you? What if you approached the Eucharist as the most important moment of your week? What if you loved others, forgave others, and served others believing anything you did for them, you did for Jesus in His most vulnerable moments?

If everything the Catholic Church teaches is true, then it's not just about going to church on Sundays, and it's not just about following a set of rules.

It's an incredible gift. An incomprehensible blessing. A striking alternative to the meaninglessness secularism offers. It's an invitation to live a life of meaning and purpose, rooted in the reality of God's incredible plan for you. And the fruits of living this way are found in the lives of the saints: peace, even in the midst of chaos and turmoil; joy, even in the midst of suffering; a heart that loves and aches compassionately for others; and a soul that delights in anything that is good, true, right, just, and noble.

In a culture that is dehumanizing people in a thousand different ways, Catholicism seeks to restore the very best of our humanity, ennobling us to live as children of God.

So, what if it's all true? The question isn't whether it will change your life. The question is: Are you ready to let it?

For three years, I answered questions for a young man who was considering becoming Catholic. He had new objections every month. Finally, I got frustrated. Not because I felt he was wasting my time, but because I felt he was wasting his time. So, this was my advice to him—and it is my advice to you today: "Live as if everything the Catholic Church teaches is true for a few months. Stop thinking about it and start living it. Live as if it were all true. That will change your life, and more importantly, it will transform you into a deeply compassionate, thoughtful, generous, loving person who is living with astounding intention."

That was seven years ago, and he has never looked back. I don't think you will either. Live as if it were all true and the fruits will speak for themselves.

Trust. Surrender. Believe. Receive.

LESSON

Live as if everything the Catholic Church teaches is true for a few months. Stop thinking about it and start living it. Live as if it were all true. That will change your life, and more importantly, it will transform you into a deeply compassionate, thoughtful, generous, loving person who is living with astounding intention. G.K. Chesterton observed, "Christianity has not been tried and found wanting. It has been found difficult and left untried." Have you ever wholeheartedly embraced Catholicism? Most people haven't. This, right now, is your moment. Don't squander it.

VIRTUE OF THE DAY

Awe: The virtue of awe is a profound respect and reverence for the source of all life. Contemplation of life, truth, beauty, goodness and the sheer power of God all nurture the virtue of awe.

DIVINE MERCY PRAYER

Eternal God, in whom mercy is endless and the treasury of compassion inexhaustible, look kindly upon us and increase Your mercy in us, that in difficult moments we might not despair nor become despondent, but with great confidence submit ourselves to Your holy will, which is Love and Mercy itself.

DAY 30
THE SACRAMENT OF MERCY

"The Lord is kind and merciful, slow to anger and abounding in steadfast love." Psalm 103:8

The Sacrament of Confession is one of the most extraordinary gifts God has given humanity. Often called the Sacrament of Mercy, it's not just about confessing sins and it's not an exercise in self-loathing. Far from it, it's about encountering God's infinite love in a deeply personal way, so that we can be set free from the mistakes of our past.

If we really understood this incredible opportunity, we would go a lot more often and with much more enthusiasm. Confession isn't a burden. It's not a chore. It's a healing encounter with the God who loves you more than you can imagine.

Though it's worth trying to imagine. Who is the one person you have loved more than any other person in this life? Immerse yourself in recollections of your love for that person. Now add to that reservoir of your love all the love you have ever had for anyone in this life. Your own reservoir of love is great. But now multiply all your love by infinity and you will have barely a glimpse of God's love.

Confession is an invitation to fully immerse yourself in God's love.

Remember, mercy is love reaching out to misery. Sin is a form of misery. Every sin leads to misery, sooner or later. And our sins create misery for others too. I don't say any of this to make you feel bad about yourself. These are just facts and reality. And no matter how much we have tried to avoid them, justify our sins, and run from God's plan—they remain true.

Our need for mercy is great. When was the last time you truly experienced mercy? Not the kind that's offered casually or half-heartedly, but soul-deep mercy that looks at your faults and failures and says, "You are still worthy of love. Your future will be better than your past." That's what happens in Confession.

Many people avoid the Sacrament of Confession because they feel shame, fear, or unworthiness. The beautiful irony is that in our unworthiness God's mercy shines brightest. When you step into the confessional, you are not met with judgment—you are met with grace, amazing grace. You're not there to dwell on your sins. You're there to leave them behind and embrace the freedom God desires for you.

Our love of comfort often keeps us from the uncomfortable spiritual experience that we desperately need.

Consider this: God already knows everything you've done, and still He invites you to bring your sins to Him and to speak them aloud. Why? It's genius. This sacrament engages and heals every aspect of the human person: physical, emotional, intellectual, spiritual, and psychological.

Acknowledging our sins, saying them out loud, is cleansing, therapeutic, cathartic, and profoundly spiritually healing. And hearing the words of absolution is not just a reminder of God's forgiveness, it is the actual moment of healing, setting you free. And who is it that forgives? "God, the Father of mercies."

Reflect for a moment on the joyful words of absolution, *"God, the Father of mercies, through the Death and Resurrection of his Son has reconciled the world to himself and poured out the Holy Spirit for the forgiveness of sins. I absolve you from your sins in the name of the Father, and of the Son, and of the Holy Spirit."*

This Sacrament of Mercy also provides a moment of piercing clarity. In the quiet of examining your conscience, you come face-to-face with two realities: who you are today and who God is calling you to become. These two visions are a natural call to change, grow, and improve. Just becoming aware of who we are and who we are capable of being challenges us to change. The sacrament allows you to let go of the guilt, regret, and shame you've been carrying so that God's mercy can renew you.

Pilgrims of Mercy unburden themselves of any unnecessary baggage. Imagine living without the weight of regret. Imagine knowing that every time you fall, there is a place to start again. That's the gift of Confession. It is the Sacrament of Mercy, the door to God's forgiveness, and a reminder that no sin is greater than His love.

Confession is love reaching out to misery. So, when was the last time you went to Confession? It's time to experience the freedom and joy that comes from encountering God's mercy. Don't wait. He is waiting for you, ready to welcome you with open arms. That's the promise of the Sacrament of Mercy. Will you accept His abundant mercy?

Trust. Surrender. Believe. Receive.

LESSON

Confession isn't a burden. It's not a chore. It's a healing encounter with the God who loves you more than you can imagine. It is the Sacrament of Mercy. An open, honest, and thorough Confession is proof that humility is starting to take root in our souls. Regular Confession is proof of our commitment to spiritual growth.

VIRTUE OF THE DAY
Honesty: The virtue of honesty involves a rigorous commitment to the truth in thought, word, and deed. Be honest with yourself—this is the first step to all personal and spiritual growth. Be honest with others—this is the key to genuine and flourishing relationships.

DIVINE MERCY PRAYER
Eternal God, in whom mercy is endless and the treasury of compassion inexhaustible, look kindly upon us and increase Your mercy in us, that in difficult moments we might not despair nor become despondent, but with great confidence submit ourselves to Your holy will, which is Love and Mercy itself.

DAY 31
BECOMING A PILGRIM OF MERCY

"The Lord is kind and merciful, slow to anger and abounding in steadfast love." Psalm 103:8

Place a bucket under a dripping faucet and it will eventually overflow. It has no choice. Once we open ourselves to receiving God's mercy, He will fill us with His love, grace, and mercy—and we too will overflow.

Once you experience the overwhelming reality of God's mercy, everything changes. It's impossible to encounter His boundless compassion without being transformed. When you truly open your heart and allow His mercy to renew you, a fire ignites within—a fire that compels you to share His mercy with the world.

This is the natural path of mercy. We spoke toward the beginning of our journey about the four movements of God's symphony of mercy.

The First Movement: Becoming Aware of Your Need for Mercy
The Second Movement: Opening Your Heart to Mercy
The Third Movement: Being Transformed by Mercy
The Fourth Movement: Becoming a Pilgrim of Mercy

When we first become aware of our need for mercy it can be overwhelming. The moment you recognize your own brokenness and your desperate need for grace, it can feel humbling, even unsettling, to honestly confront your flaws. But that's where mercy begins—not in judgment, but in love. And once you experience that love, it's no longer just about you. Mercy changes your perspective. It opens your eyes to the pain, suffering, and woundedness of those around you.

This is where the call to be a Pilgrim of Mercy becomes clear. You realize that God's mercy was never meant to stop with you. It's a gift to be shared—a force that yearns to go forth, bringing healing and hope to others. Being a Pilgrim of Mercy doesn't require you to travel to foreign lands. It begins with your everyday interactions. It's as simple as being patient with a difficult person by realizing that the way he behaves is an expression of a wound he is carrying. Or as ordinary as offering to help another person who seems overwhelmed rather than rushing to get to the next activity on our schedule. It may involve forgiving a friend who has hurt you or reaching out to someone who you know is lonely. Our days are full of opportunities to share God's mercy with other people—to be Pilgrims of Mercy.

Here's the beautiful thing: As you extend mercy to others, you deepen your own experience of God's mercy. It's a cycle of grace—the giving and receiving go hand in hand. Through this process you become a living witness to the power of mercy, forgiveness, goodness, and love.

Becoming a Pilgrim of Mercy doesn't mean you have all the answers or that you're perfect. It's your imperfections and your own need for God's mercy that qualify you. You are simply sharing what you have received, trusting that God will work through you. And He will. Make yourself available to God and He will work wonders through you.

Imagine a world where we all participate in these cycles of mercy and grace—a world where forgiveness replaces resentment, where kindness heals divisions, and where love triumphs over judgment. That's the power of mercy. That's the world God imagined when He sent His Son Jesus to set off an everlasting chain reaction of mercy.

Are you willing to allow God's mercy to flow through you to others? You know from your own experience that a little mercy can make a significant difference. And you know how desperately the world needs God's mercy. News from around the world screams out for mercy. The world and the devil want you to believe that you can't do anything about it, that your efforts are insignificant, but these are obvious lies. You can't do everything, but you can do your part, and that is all that is expected of you. So, let's go out into this broken world each day looking for opportunities to be Pilgrims of Mercy.

Trust. Surrender. Believe. Receive.

LESSON

Every moment is an opportunity to share God's mercy with others, and every moment of mercy is a Holy Moment. Some moments are holy, some moments are unholy, and you get to decide. Fill your life with Holy Moments, one at a time.

VIRTUE OF THE DAY
Simplicity: The virtue of simplicity fosters a spirit of contentment. Never confuse needs with wants. Concern yourself with the essential few rather than the trivial many. Liberate yourself from the things of this world so that your heart is free to rejoice in the pursuit of holiness.

DIVINE MERCY PRAYER
Eternal God, in whom mercy is endless and the treasury of compassion inexhaustible, look kindly upon us and increase Your mercy in us, that in difficult moments we might not despair nor become despondent, but with great confidence submit ourselves to Your holy will, which is Love and Mercy itself.

DAY 32
GIFT OF PEACE

"The Lord is kind and merciful, slow to anger and abounding in steadfast love." Psalm 103:8

It's a grotesque analogy, but one we will all understand. Imagine someone deposited billions of dollars into a bank account for you, but you never went to the bank to access any of it. Imagine you had billions of dollars in the bank but were living on the streets and starving. This is the relationship we have with the peace that Jesus left us.

Jesus said, "My peace I give you, my peace I leave you." (John 14:27) Everyone I know would like a deeper sense of peace. We have all thought or said things like, "I just need a little peace and quiet." We're right. We need a little peace and quiet.

Now, imagine how vast the peace of God is. This peace is your birthright. It's your inheritance as a child of God. But we treat it like having billions of dollars in the bank and never stopping by to make a withdrawal so we can use it for ourselves and others.

The peace of Christ is not like the fleeting calm we experience when life is easy or the temporary relief when a problem is solved. It is something far greater—an unshakable peace that can steady us through any storm.

Imagine if we truly embodied the peace of Christ in our daily lives. How would we live differently? We would no longer be consumed with anxiety over things beyond our control. The peace of Christ reminds us that God holds us lovingly in the palm of His hands, that He is with us in every moment, and that His love is greater than any challenge we face. This peace liberates us from worry and allows us to live with trust and confidence.

This peace would also transform our relationships. When we embody the peace of Christ, we are less likely to react with anger, frustration, or impatience. A peace-filled Christian approaches others with compassion, gentleness, understanding, and love.

When people spend time with you, do they settle into a deep peaceful feeling? Do their anxieties fade into the background? Do they breathe a little easier? Do their burdens feel a little lighter?

Christ's peace becomes the foundation for building stronger, more compassionate communities. A peace-filled Christian listens more deeply, forgives more freely, and prefers unity to division.

On a personal level, the peace of Christ provides personal clarity about who we are, what we are here for, what matters most, and what matters least.

The peace of Jesus liberates us from all the distraction and chaos around us by providing an extraordinary inner calm.

The people of our age are restless, anxious, agitated, fidgety, tense, unsettled, on edge, jittery, impatient, depressed, uneasy, frazzled, distracted, nervous, worried, fearful, stressed, overwhelmed, apprehensive—and in desperate need of God's gift of peace.

Mercy always precedes peace. When the priest or deacon says in the Mass, "Let us offer each other the sign of peace" we have already begged God for His mercy with the *Kyrie* during the Penitential Rite. Without mercy there cannot be peace in our hearts. Peace is the fruit of mercy.

And the peace Jesus gives us is contagious. He fills us with His peace and sends us out on mission as Pilgrims of Mercy. One of the most famous prayers in Christian history is the prayer of Saint Francis of Assisi.

Lord, make me an instrument of your peace.
Where there is hatred, let me sow love;
where there is injury, pardon;
where there is doubt, faith;
where there is despair, hope;
where there is darkness, light;
and where there is sadness, joy.

O Divine Master, grant that I may not so much seek
to be consoled as to console;
to be understood as to understand;
to be loved as to love.
For it is in giving that we receive;
it is in pardoning that we are pardoned;
and it is in dying that we are born to eternal life.

Amen.

When we embody the peace of Christ we become instruments of peace in a restless world. Our presence becomes a calming force, a reminder that true peace is possible.

So, how would your life change if you fully embraced the peace Jesus offers? Imagine a life where fear no longer holds you back, where love flows freely, and where joy becomes your default state. That's the promise of Christ's peace—a gift He is waiting for you to accept.

And how do we access the peace Jesus offers us? You stay warm by staying close to the fire. Stay close to Jesus and you will live in His peace.

Jesus said, "My peace I give you, my peace I leave you." Let's choose to live in that peace and share that peace with others today.

Trust. Surrender. Believe. Receive.

LESSON

Jesus said, "My peace I give you, my peace I leave you." (John 14:27) His peace liberates us from all the distraction and chaos around us by providing calm direction. You stay warm by staying close to the fire. Stay close to Jesus and you will live in His peace. When we embody the peace of Christ we become instruments of peace in a restless world.

VIRTUE OF THE DAY

Peace: The virtue of peace allows us to remain calm in the face of chaos and focused when life seems overwhelming. Peace is a gift from God that can manifest in a myriad of ways internally and externally. Be respectful. Let your language reflect the peace of your soul. Avoid violence. Look for peaceful solutions to problems.

DIVINE MERCY PRAYER

Eternal God, in whom mercy is endless and the treasury of compassion inexhaustible, look kindly upon us and increase Your mercy in us, that in difficult moments we might not despair nor become despondent, but with great confidence submit ourselves to Your holy will, which is Love and Mercy itself.

DAY 33
JESUS, I TRUST IN YOU

"The Lord is kind and merciful, slow to anger and abounding in steadfast love." Psalm 103:8

Today is a historic moment in your life and the end of our journey. We have been on this path together for thirty-three days. Congratulations! You did it. I am sure there are many who didn't make it. We pray they will get back on the path and complete this Divine Mercy consecration soon. But today is your day. I hope you will find a way to celebrate it.

This consecration is a radical act of love. It is an act of radical generosity. Deep down we all desire to make the radical and complete gift of self that you are going to make to God today.

Saint Anthony of Padua advises you today, "By His whole self He redeemed your whole self, so that He alone might possess you wholly. Therefore, love the Lord your God with all your heart. Do not withhold even the smallest part of yourself. Love wholly, not in part."

Today you are offering your whole self to Jesus. Don't hold anything back. Your consecration is a declaration before God. You are joining your "yes" with Mary's "yes," with Joseph's "yes," with the "yes" of the disciples, and the "yes" of all the angels and saints throughout history.

Consecration to Divine Mercy is a life-changing act of surrender. It's not just a prayer or a devotion. It's a commitment to place your life, your hopes, dreams, relationships, career, and your struggles in the hands of Jesus with complete trust. At the heart of this consecration is a simple yet profound declaration: *"Jesus, I trust in You."*

What does it mean to trust in Jesus? Trust isn't passive, it's active. It's a daily decision to believe that Jesus is with you, guiding you, and working for your good, even when life feels uncertain.

What is our biggest obstacle to trusting Jesus in our modern culture? Our delusional and disordered desire to control everything. Trust means letting go of the need to control everything and instead relying on His wisdom and providence.

It's easy to say, but in practice, trust often requires us to face our fears, release our anxieties, and step into the unknown with faith.

When you consecrate yourself to Divine Mercy, you are saying, *"Jesus, I trust that Your mercy is greater than my sins. I trust that Your plan is better than mine. I trust that You will never abandon me, no matter what life throws my way."* This trust transforms the way you live. It gives you peace when you are confused, courage when you face challenges, and preserves your hope in life's darkest moments.

The rays of light streaming from Jesus' heart in the image of Divine Mercy symbolize the ocean of mercy flowing from His Sacred Heart. That is the ocean of mercy that He offers to each of us. But like any gift, mercy must be received. Humility opens the door of our hearts. Trust allows His mercy to restructure our lives. You see, our lives don't need a small shift here and a tweak there, they need to be completely restructured to allow His mercy to fill our hearts, heal our wounds, and guide us on the path to holiness.

The endless mercy of Jesus transforms the way we treat others too. Place a bucket under a dripping faucet and it will eventually overflow. It has no choice. As we allow Jesus to fill our hearts with mercy, we become channels of His compassion and love, reminding others that they, too, can place their trust in Him.

"*Jesus, I trust in You.*" These five words can change your life. They invite you into a deeper relationship with Jesus. This Divine Mercy consecration is an invitation to live with unwavering trust in the One who holds all things in His hands—and the plans He has for you and your life.

Amazing things become possible when we surrender ourselves unreservedly to Jesus, and that is exactly what you are going to do today by consecrating yourself to Jesus, the Divine Mercy.

This is a moment of amazing grace.

Amazing grace! How sweet the sound
That saved a wretch like me!
I once was lost, but now am found;
Was blind, but now I see.

Haven't we all felt wretched at times? Don't we all need to be saved? We've all been lost, we may be lost right now, but His grace and mercy will lead us home. And we are all blind in so many ways, but His mercy is opening our eyes.

"*The Lord has promised good to me. . .*" and to you.

It's time to open our hearts to His endless goodness. It is goodness that we desire.

The goodness of God is available to everyone, everywhere, and at all times. Isn't it time, once and for all, to turn away from the meaninglessness of our age and live a deeply meaningful life? You cannot live a deeply meaningful life by filling your life with meaningless things and activities. Isn't it time, once and for all, to turn away from all the seductive shiny things of this world and fill our lives with God and all His goodness?

Divine Mercy heals us and prepares us for mission.

Allow Jesus, the Divine Mercy, to fill your life with love, compassion, kindness, gratitude, and a boundless generosity. Take risks with your goodness. Go beyond your self-imposed comfortable boundaries. Test the limits of your goodness. Find new horizons of possibility. Don't just love people, astonish people with your love. Don't just dabble in generosity, live a life of staggering generosity. Don't just set out to do a little good in this world when it's convenient and an opportunity arises. Go out of your way to find astonishingly inconvenient opportunities to fill this world with goodness.

And now it is time to consecrate ourselves to Jesus Christ, the Divine Mercy.

Trust. Surrender. Believe. Receive.

Congratulations!
Download your FREE Commemorative Consecration Certificate! Visit **www.PilgrimsofMercy.com/4** or scan the QR code!

DIVINE MERCY CONSECRATION PRAYER

Lord Jesus Christ,
True God and True Man,
Bread of Life,
The Alpha and the Omega,
Beloved Son of God and Love Incarnate,
the Divine Mercy,
I consecrate myself to You today
without reservation.

I come before You today as I am,
weak, wounded, and broken,
but hopeful,
and yearning for Your mercy.
Remind me that I am a child of God,
first and foremost.
Heal the wounds of my past,
guide my feet in the present,
and protect my future with Your care and provision.
Show me what is possible when I trust in You.
Free me from the guilt, shame, regret, and insecurity
that prevent me from fully embracing Your promises.

Lord Jesus Christ,
Face of the Father's Mercy,
Lamb of God who takes away the sins of the world,
I consecrate myself to Your Divine Mercy today
without reservation.
I hold nothing back.

I surrender completely and absolutely to Your goodness.
There is nothing I can do to make You love me.
There is nothing I can do to lose Your love.
All that is left is to receive graciously
that which I don't deserve but can't live without.
I open my heart to You in trust and surrender.
Fill my heart with Your Divine Mercy until it overflows.

Jesus,
Lord of Mercy,
I stand before You today with an open heart.
Everything is on the table.
Take what You want to take,
and give what You want to give.
When Your mercy is uncomfortable, difficult, or inconvenient,
remind me that Your mercy
is always an invitation to
a better life.

Lord Jesus Christ,
Prince of Peace,
I consecrate myself to You today without reservation.
Fill my life with radical love,
tender compassion,
gentle kindness,
endless gratitude,
and boundless generosity.
Send me out into the world as a Pilgrim of Mercy.

Mary,
Mother of Mercy,
You stood at the foot of the Cross
as blood and water poured from your Son's side
to bathe the world in mercy.
Teach me to trust wholeheartedly
in God's unfathomable
plans for my life
today, tomorrow, and forever!

Jesus, I trust in You!

Amen.

APPENDIX

THE DIVINE MERCY CHAPLET

The Divine Mercy Chaplet is a powerful way to ask Jesus for mercy and love and was popularized by Saint Faustina. People typically use rosary beads to guide them as they pray for the world, people close to death, or any other special intentions.

How to Pray the Divine Mercy Chaplet

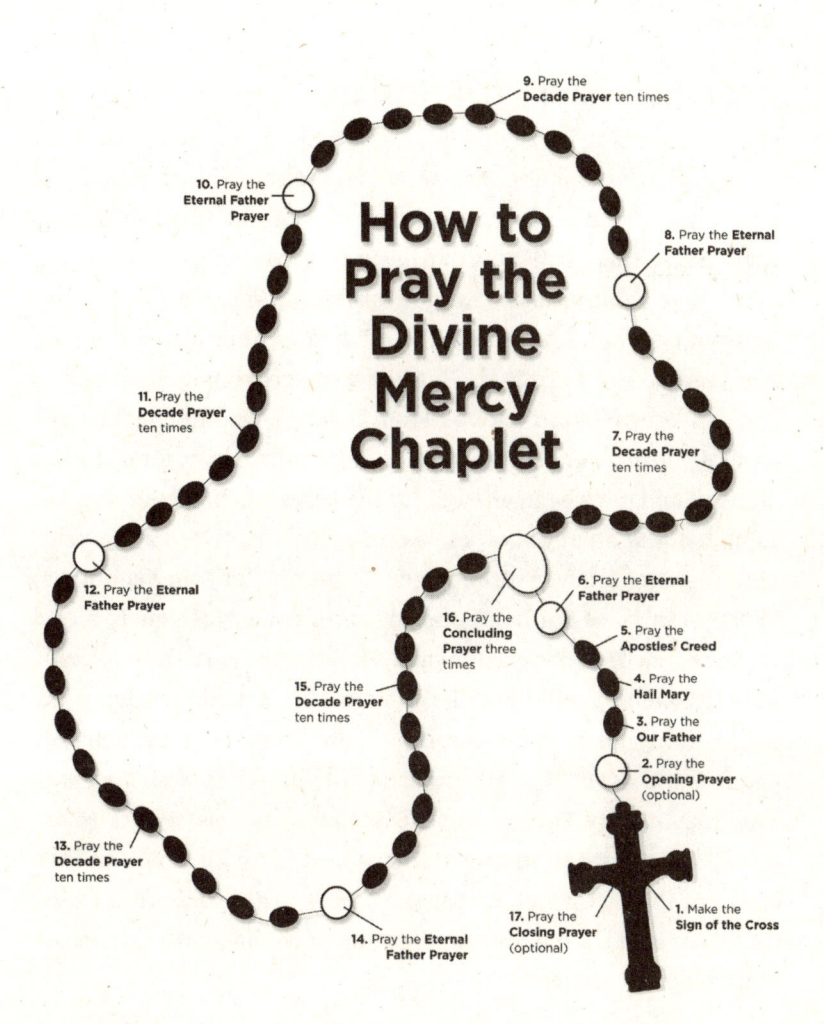

1. Make the **Sign of the Cross**
2. Pray the **Opening Prayer** (optional)
3. Pray the **Our Father**
4. Pray the **Hail Mary**
5. Pray the **Apostles' Creed**
6. Pray the **Eternal Father Prayer**
7. Pray the **Decade Prayer** ten times
8. Pray the **Eternal Father Prayer**
9. Pray the **Decade Prayer** ten times
10. Pray the **Eternal Father Prayer**
11. Pray the **Decade Prayer** ten times
12. Pray the **Eternal Father Prayer**
13. Pray the **Decade Prayer** ten times
14. Pray the **Eternal Father Prayer**
15. Pray the **Decade Prayer** ten times
16. Pray the **Concluding Prayer** three times
17. Pray the **Closing Prayer** (optional)

THE SIGN OF THE CROSS
In the name of the Father, and of the Son, and of the Holy Spirit. Amen.

OPENING PRAYER (OPTIONAL)
O Jesus, eternal Truth, our Life, I call upon You and I beg Your mercy for poor sinners. O sweetest Heart of my Lord, full of pity and unfathomable mercy, I plead with You for poor sinners. O Most Sacred Heart, Fount of Mercy from which gush forth rays of inconceivable graces upon the entire human race, I beg of You light for poor sinners. O Jesus, be mindful of Your own bitter Passion and do not permit the loss of souls redeemed at so dear a price of Your most precious Blood. O Jesus, when I consider the great price of Your Blood, I rejoice at its immensity, for one drop alone would have been enough for the salvation of all sinners. Although sin is an abyss of wickedness and ingratitude, the price paid for us can never be equaled. Therefore, let every soul trust in the Passion of the Lord, and place its hope in His mercy. God will not deny His mercy to anyone. Heaven and earth may change, but God's mercy will never be exhausted. Oh, what immense joy burns in my heart when I contemplate Your incomprehensible goodness, O Jesus! I desire to bring all sinners to Your feet that they may glorify Your mercy throughout endless ages. You expired, Jesus, but the source of life gushed forth for souls, and the ocean of mercy opened up for the whole world. O Fount of Life, unfathomable Divine Mercy, envelop the whole world and empty Yourself out upon us.

Repeat Three Times: O Blood and Water, which gushed forth from the Heart of Jesus as a fount of mercy for us, I trust in You!

THE OUR FATHER

Our Father, who art in heaven, hallowed be Thy name; Thy kingdom come; Thy will be done on earth as it is in heaven. Give us this day our daily bread; and forgive us our trespasses as we forgive those who trespass against us; and lead us not into temptation, but deliver us from evil. Amen.

THE HAIL MARY

Hail Mary, full of grace. The Lord is with thee. Blessed art thou amongst women, and blessed is the fruit of thy womb, Jesus. Holy Mary, Mother of God, pray for us sinners, now and at the hour of our death. Amen.

THE APOSTLES' CREED

I believe in God, the Father Almighty, Creator of heaven and earth; and in Jesus Christ, His only Son, our Lord; who was conceived by the Holy Spirit, born of the Virgin Mary, suffered under Pontius Pilate, was crucified, died, and was buried. He descended into hell; the third day He arose again from the dead; He ascended into heaven, sits at the right hand of God, the Father Almighty; from thence He shall come to judge the living and the dead. I believe in the Holy Spirit, the Holy Catholic Church, the communion of saints, the forgiveness of sins, the resurrection of the body, and life everlasting. Amen.

ETERNAL FATHER

On each of the large beads, where you typically would say the "Our Father," pray: Eternal Father, I offer You the Body and Blood, Soul and Divinity of Your Dearly Beloved Son, Our Lord, Jesus Christ, in atonement for our sins and those of the whole world.

DECADE PRAYER
On the ten small beads of each decade, pray: For the sake of His sorrowful Passion, have mercy on us and on the whole world.

REPEAT THIS PATTERN FOR A TOTAL OF FIVE DECADES
For each decade: Begin with the "Eternal Father" prayer, and then pray, "For the sake of His sorrowful passion..." ten times.

CONCLUDING PRAYER
Repeat three times: Holy God, Holy Mighty One, Holy Immortal One, have mercy on us and on the whole world.

CLOSING PRAYERS (OPTIONAL)
Eternal God, in whom mercy is endless and the treasury of compassion inexhaustible, look kindly upon us and increase Your mercy in us, that in difficult moments we might not despair nor become despondent, but with great confidence submit ourselves to Your holy will, which is Love and Mercy itself.

O Greatly Merciful God, Infinite Goodness, today all mankind calls out from the abyss of its misery to Your mercy—to Your compassion, O God; and it is with its mighty voice of misery that it cries out. Gracious God, do not reject the prayer of this earth's exiles! O Lord, Goodness beyond our understanding, Who are acquainted with our misery through and through, and know that by our own power we cannot ascend to You, we implore You: anticipate us with Your grace and keep on increasing Your mercy in us, that we may faithfully do Your holy will all through our life and at death's hour. Let the omnipotence of Your mercy shield us from the darts of our salvation's enemies, that we may with confidence, as Your children, await Your [Son's] final coming—that day known to You alone. And we expect to obtain everything promised us by Jesus in spite of all our wretchedness. For Jesus is our Hope: through His merciful Heart, as through an open gate, we pass through to heaven. (Diary, 1570)

THE SIGN OF THE CROSS
In the name of the Father, and of the Son, and of the Holy Spirit. Amen.

THE DIVINE MERCY NOVENA

The Divine Mercy Novena is a special prayer said over the course of nine days that asks Jesus to bless the world with His Divine Mercy. Jesus taught Faustina this special novena and said: "I will deny nothing to any soul whom you will bring to the fount of My mercy." (Diary, 1209) You can pray the Divine Mercy novena any time of year, but traditionally the Church prays it for nine days from Good Friday to Divine Mercy Sunday.

DAY 1

"Today bring to Me ALL MANKIND, ESPECIALLY ALL SINNERS, and immerse them in the ocean of My mercy. In this way you will console Me in the bitter grief into which the loss of souls plunges Me."

Most Merciful Jesus, whose very nature it is to have compassion on us and to forgive us, do not look upon our sins but upon our trust which we place in Your infinite goodness. Receive us all into the abode of Your Most Compassionate Heart, and never let us escape from It. We beg this of You by Your love which unites You to the Father and the Holy Spirit.

Eternal Father, turn Your merciful gaze upon all mankind and especially upon poor sinners, all enfolded in the Most Compassionate Heart of Jesus. For the sake of His sorrowful Passion show us Your mercy, that we may praise the omnipotence of Your mercy for ever and ever. Amen

Conclusion: Pray the Divine Mercy Chaplet.

DAY 2

"Today bring to Me THE SOULS OF PRIESTS AND RELIGIOUS, and immerse them in My unfathomable mercy. It was they who gave Me strength to endure My bitter Passion. Through them as through channels My mercy flows out upon mankind."

Most Merciful Jesus, from whom comes all that is good, increase Your grace in men and women consecrated to Your service, that they may perform worthy works of mercy; and that all who see them may glorify the Father of Mercy who is in Heaven.

Eternal Father, turn Your merciful gaze upon the company of chosen ones in Your vineyard—upon the souls of priests and religious; and endow them with the strength of Your blessing. For the love of the Heart of Your Son in which they are enfolded, impart to them Your power and light, that they may be able to guide others in the way of salvation and with one voice sing praise to Your boundless mercy for ages without end. Amen.

Conclusion: Pray the Divine Mercy Chaplet.

DAY 3

"Today bring to Me ALL DEVOUT AND FAITHFUL SOULS, and immerse them in the ocean of My mercy. These souls brought Me consolation on the Way of the Cross. They were that drop of consolation in the midst of an ocean of bitterness."

Most Merciful Jesus, from the treasury of Your mercy, You impart Your graces in great abundance to each and all. Receive us into the abode of Your Most Compassionate Heart and never let us escape from It. We beg this grace of You by that most wondrous love for the heavenly Father with which Your Heart burns so fiercely.

Eternal Father, turn Your merciful gaze upon faithful souls, as upon the inheritance of Your Son. For the sake of His sorrowful Passion, grant them Your blessing and surround them with Your constant protection. Thus may they never fail in love or lose the treasure of the holy faith, but rather, with all the hosts of Angels and Saints, may they glorify Your boundless mercy for endless ages. Amen.

Conclusion: Pray the Divine Mercy Chaplet.

DAY 4

"Today bring to Me THOSE WHO DO NOT BELIEVE IN GOD AND THOSE WHO DO NOT YET KNOW ME. I was thinking also of them during My bitter Passion, and their future zeal comforted My Heart. Immerse them in the ocean of My mercy."

Most compassionate Jesus, You are the Light of the whole world. Receive into the abode of Your Most Compassionate Heart the souls of those who do not believe in God and of those who as yet do not know You. Let the rays of Your grace enlighten them that they, too, together with us, may extol Your wonderful mercy; and do not let them escape from the abode which is Your Most Compassionate Heart.

Eternal Father, turn Your merciful gaze upon the souls of those who do not believe in You, and of those who as yet do not know You, but who are enclosed in the Most Compassionate Heart of Jesus. Draw them to the light of the Gospel. These souls do not know what great happiness it is to love You. Grant that they, too, may extol the generosity of Your mercy for endless ages. Amen.

Conclusion: Pray the Divine Mercy Chaplet.

DAY 5

"Today bring to Me THE SOULS OF THOSE WHO HAVE SEPARATED THEMSELVES FROM MY CHURCH, and immerse them in the ocean of My mercy. During My bitter Passion they tore at My Body and Heart, that is, My Church. As they return to unity with the Church, My wounds heal and in this way they alleviate My Passion."

Most Merciful Jesus, Goodness Itself, You do not refuse light to those who seek it of You. Receive into the abode of Your Most Compassionate Heart the souls of those who have separated themselves from Your Church. Draw them by Your light into the unity of the Church, and do not let them escape from the abode of Your Most Compassionate Heart; but bring it about that they, too, come to glorify the generosity of Your mercy.

Eternal Father, turn Your merciful gaze upon the souls of those who have separated themselves from Your Son's Church, who have squandered Your blessings and misused Your graces by obstinately persisting in their errors. Do not look upon their errors, but upon the love of Your own Son and upon His bitter Passion, which He underwent for their sake, since they, too, are enclosed in His Most Compassionate Heart. Bring it about that they also may glorify Your great mercy for endless ages. Amen.

Conclusion: Pray the Divine Mercy Chaplet.

DAY 6

"Today bring to Me THE MEEK AND HUMBLE SOULS AND THE SOULS OF LITTLE CHILDREN, and immerse them in My mercy. These souls most closely resemble My Heart. They strengthened Me during My bitter agony. I saw them as earthly Angels, who will keep vigil at My altars. I pour out upon them whole torrents of grace. Only the humble soul is capable of receiving My grace. I favor humble souls with My confidence."

Most Merciful Jesus, You yourself have said, "Learn from Me for I am meek and humble of heart." Receive into the abode of Your Most Compassionate Heart all meek and humble souls and the souls of little children. These souls send all heaven into ecstasy and they are the heavenly Father's favorites. They are a sweet-smelling bouquet before the throne of God; God Himself takes delight in their fragrance. These souls have a permanent abode in Your Most Compassionate Heart, O Jesus, and they unceasingly sing out a hymn of love and mercy.

Eternal Father, turn Your merciful gaze upon meek souls, upon humble souls, and upon little children who are enfolded in the abode which is the Most Compassionate Heart of Jesus. These souls bear the closest resemblance to Your Son. Their fragrance rises from the earth and reaches Your very throne. Father of mercy and of all goodness, I beg You by the love You bear these souls and by the delight You take in them: Bless the whole world, that all souls together may sing out the praises of Your mercy for endless ages. Amen

Conclusion: **Pray the Divine Mercy Chaplet.**

DAY 7

"Today bring to Me THE SOULS WHO ESPECIALLY VENERATE AND GLORIFY MY MERCY, and immerse them in My mercy. These souls sorrowed most over my Passion and entered most deeply into My spirit. They are living images of My Compassionate Heart. These souls will shine with a special brightness in the next life. Not one of them will go into the fire of hell. I shall particularly defend each one of them at the hour of death."

Most Merciful Jesus, whose Heart is Love Itself, receive into the abode of Your Most Compassionate Heart the souls of those who particularly extol and venerate the greatness of Your mercy. These souls are mighty with the very power of God Himself. In the midst of all afflictions and adversities they go forward, confident of Your mercy; and united to You, O Jesus, they carry all mankind on their shoulders. These souls will not be judged severely, but Your mercy will embrace them as they depart from this life.

Eternal Father, turn Your merciful gaze upon the souls who glorify and venerate Your greatest attribute, that of Your fathomless mercy, and who are enclosed in the Most Compassionate Heart of Jesus. These souls are a living Gospel; their hands are full of deeds of mercy, and their hearts, overflowing with joy, sing a canticle of mercy to You, O Most High! I beg You O God: Show them Your mercy according to the hope and trust they have placed in You. Let there be accomplished in them the promise of Jesus, who said to them, I Myself will defend as My own glory, during their lifetime, and especially at the hour of their death, those souls who will venerate My fathomless mercy. Amen.

Conclusion: Pray the Divine Mercy Chaplet.

DAY 8

"Today bring to Me THE SOULS WHO ARE DETAINED IN PURGATORY, and immerse them in the abyss of My mercy. Let the torrents of My Blood cool down their scorching flames. All these souls are greatly loved by Me. They are making retribution to My justice. It is in your power to bring them relief. Draw all the indulgences from the treasury of My Church and offer them on their behalf. Oh, if you only knew the torments they suffer, you would continually offer for them the alms of the spirit and pay off their debt to My justice."

Most Merciful Jesus, You Yourself have said that You desire mercy; so I bring into the abode of Your Most Compassionate Heart the souls in Purgatory, souls who are very dear to You, and yet, who must make retribution to Your justice. May the streams of Blood and Water which gushed forth from Your Heart put out the flames of Purgatory, that there, too, the power of Your mercy may be celebrated.

Eternal Father, turn Your merciful gaze upon the souls suffering in Purgatory, who are enfolded in the Most Compassionate Heart of Jesus. I beg You, by the sorrowful Passion of Jesus Your Son, and by all the bitterness with which His most sacred Soul was flooded: Manifest Your mercy to the souls who are under Your just scrutiny. Look upon them in no other way but only through the Wounds of Jesus, Your dearly beloved Son; for we firmly believe that there is no limit to Your goodness and compassion. Amen.

Conclusion: Pray the Divine Mercy Chaplet.

DAY 9

"Today bring to Me SOULS WHO HAVE BECOME LUKEWARM, and immerse them in the abyss of My mercy. These souls wound My Heart most painfully. My soul suffered the most dreadful loathing in the Garden of Olives because of lukewarm souls. They were the reason I cried out: 'Father, take this cup away from Me, if it be Your will.' For them, the last hope of salvation is to run to My mercy."

Most compassionate Jesus, You are Compassion Itself. I bring lukewarm souls into the abode of Your Most Compassionate Heart. In this fire of Your pure love, let these tepid souls, who, like corpses, filled You with such deep loathing, be once again set aflame. O Most Compassionate Jesus, exercise the omnipotence of Your mercy and draw them into the very ardor of Your love, and bestow upon them the gift of holy love, for nothing is beyond Your power.

Eternal Father, turn Your merciful gaze upon lukewarm souls who are nonetheless enfolded in the Most Compassionate Heart of Jesus. Father of Mercy, I beg You by the bitter Passion of Your Son and by His three-hour agony on the Cross: Let them, too, glorify the abyss of Your mercy. Amen.

Conclusion: Pray the Divine Mercy Chaplet.

DIVINE MERCY AND THE SACRED HEART DEVOTION

Devotion to the Sacred Heart of Jesus is devotion to Jesus Himself—specifically His heart, which is overwhelmed with love and mercy for God and all mankind.

Pope Pius XII put it this way, "The Heart of the Incarnate Word is deservedly and rightly considered the chief sign and symbol of that... love with which the divine Redeemer unceasingly loves His eternal Father and all mankind."

HISTORY OF THE DEVOTION

Saint Margaret Mary Alacoque (1647–1690) was a French Visitation nun who experienced visions of Jesus. During these visions, Jesus spoke to her about His Sacred Heart as a symbol of His love and mercy for humanity.

Jesus expressed His desire for humanity to draw closer to His heart, particularly through Eucharistic devotion and reparation for sins. This led Pope Pius IX to institute of the Feast of the Sacred Heart on the Friday following the Feast of Corpus Christi.

The Catholic Church has both approved and recommended devotion to the Sacred Heart of Jesus as a way to grow deeper in faith and experience God's mercy anew.

CONNECTION TO DIVINE MERCY

The connections between devotion to the Sacred Heart and Divine Mercy are striking and profound. Nearly three-hundred years after Jesus appeared to Saint Margaret Mary Alacoque, He appeared to another humble nun, Saint Faustina Kowalska, to express His desire that His mercy be shared with the world.

Saint Catherine of Siena provides an image that can help us understand the connection between these two great devotions. She says that the love that flows from God's heart always crosses a bridge of mercy in order to reach the world. The Sacred Heart devotion encourages us to reflect on the love that overwhelms Jesus' heart. The Divine Mercy devotion encourages us to reflect on how that love reaches out to us in our misery.

THE SACRED HEART PRAYER
BY SAINT MARGARET MARY ALACOQUE

Lord Jesus,

Let my heart never rest until it finds You,
who are its center, its love, and its happiness.
By the wound in Your heart,
pardon the sins that I have committed
whether out of malice or out of evil desires.
Place my weak heart in Your own divine heart,
continually under Your protection and guidance,
so that I may persevere in doing good
and in fleeing evil until my last breath.

Amen.

COMMON SACRED HEART DEVOTIONAL PRACTICES

The Sacred Heart Devotion has led generations of Catholics to a deeper understanding of God's unconditional love and abundant mercy. There are many ways you can make this devotion a greater part of your spiritual life:

1. **Celebrate First Fridays.** On the first Friday of the month, for nine consecutive months, go to Confession and receive the Eucharist. Because of the power of this special devotion, many parishes host First Friday Masses and Confessions.

2. **Celebrate the Feast of the Sacred Heart.** This special feast day is celebrated on the Friday after the feast of Corpus Christi. You can celebrate by attending Mass, receiving the Eucharist, and spending time in prayer, meditating on the Sacred Heart.

3. **Celebrate the Month of the Sacred Heart.** The Church has dedicated the entire month of June to the Sacred Heart of Jesus. This is the perfect time to deepen your spiritual life and devotion of the Sacred Heart.

4. **Enthrone an image of the Sacred Heart in your home.** When Jesus appeared to Saint Margaret Mary, He said: "I will bless every dwelling where an image of My Heart is both exposed and honored." During an enthronement ceremony, a priest (ideally) will lead a small ceremony in your home where an image of the Sacred Heart of Jesus is placed somewhere prominent. The home, the image, and the family are all blessed. If you want to learn more about enthronement, speak to your parish priest!

PROMISES OF THE SACRED HEART DEVOTION

Jesus made many promises to those who have devotion to His Sacred Heart:

1. "I will give them all the graces necessary in their state of life.
2. I will establish peace in their homes.
3. I will comfort them in all their afflictions.
4. I will be their secure refuge during life, and above all, in death.
5. I will bestow abundant blessings upon all their undertakings.
6. Sinners will find in my Heart the source and infinite ocean of mercy.
7. Lukewarm souls shall become fervent.
8. Fervent souls shall quickly mount to high perfection.
9. I will bless every place in which an image of my Heart is exposed and honored.
10. I will give to priests the gift of touching the most hardened hearts.
11. Those who shall promote this devotion shall have their names written in my Heart.
12. I promise you in the excessive mercy of my Heart that my all-powerful love will grant to all those who receive Holy Communion on the First Fridays in nine consecutive months the grace of final perseverance; they shall not die in my disgrace, nor without receiving their sacraments. My divine Heart shall be their safe refuge in this last moment."

NOTES

NOTES

NOTES

NOTES

NOTES

NOTES

NOTES

NOTES

NOTES

NOTES

NOTES

NOTES

NOTES

NOTES

THE FIRST EUCHARISTIC CONSECRATION.
AN UNPRECEDENTED SPIRITUAL RESOURCE.

Available in Softcover, eBook, and Audiobook!

ORDER YOUR COPY TODAY AT

Eucharist.us
THE INTERNATIONAL SOCIETY OF THE EUCHARIST